Christine Ball is of Romany Gypsy background and recently lost her Husband. She also lost her Son Naylor 13 years ago in a car accident. After years of suffering from depression it has inspired her to write this book to help others.

She is a mother of three children, a grandmother of twelve and a great-grandmother of three. She currently works in a small family run deli.

There I Was: Here I Am

CHRISTINE BALL

Balboa Press books may be ordered through booksellers or by contacting:

Balboa Press
A Division of Hay House
1663 Liberty Drive
Bloomington, IN 47403
www.balboapress.com
1 (877) 407-4847

Because of the dynamic nature of the Internet, any web addresses or links contained in this book may have changed since publication and may no longer be valid. The views expressed in this work are solely those of the author and do not necessarily reflect the views of the publisher, and the publisher hereby disclaims any responsibility for them.

The author of this book does not dispense medical advice or prescribe the use of any technique as a form of treatment for physical, emotional, or medical problems without the advice of a physician, either directly or indirectly. The intent of the author is only to offer information of a general nature to help you in your quest for emotional and spiritual well-being. In the event you use any of the information in this book for yourself, which is your constitutional right, the author and the publisher assume no responsibility for your actions.

This book is a work of non-fiction. Unless otherwise noted, the author and the publisher make no explicit guarantees as to the accuracy of the information contained in this book and in some cases, names of people and places have been altered to protect their privacy.

Any people depicted in stock imagery provided by Thinkstock are models, and such images are being used for illustrative purposes only.
Certain stock imagery © Thinkstock.

Print information available on the last page.

ISBN: 978-1-5043-9036-1 (sc)
ISBN: 978-1-5043-9038-5 (hc)
ISBN: 978-1-5043-9037-8 (e)

Library of Congress Control Number: 2017917277

Balboa Press rev. date: 11/15/2017

My beautiful baby.

DEDICATION

I dedicate this book to my beautiful Son Naylor and husband Alfie. I will hold them both in my heart forever, and not forgetting my children Alfie and Phyllis, also my grandson Naylor and all my other grandchildren who I love very dearly. And so important to me all the heartbroken mothers and fathers in the world. There is no Pain deeper than the loss of a child, no one should have to suffer this Pain alone.

The 'birthday rose'.

FOREWORD

Christine needed to write this book. First, she needed to write it for herself, as a means of visualising, qualifying and ultimately dealing with her grief. Second, she needed to write this book to help others recover from the destructive power of irreplaceable loss. Christine is a person driven by the desire to help others and the second reason for the existence of this book soon overtook the first.

She is a truly remarkable woman who lives for her family and friends, and as you will see as you read this book, Christine is blessed with an incredible will to survive, recover, and go on to be who she was always meant to be. She also has a gift for communication, empathy and understanding, and this book will illustrate that. Within these pages, Christine has been open and honest to a degree some will find shocking. Romani people do not usually bare their souls as Christine has, but her book could not be what it, and she, needed it to be, without it's brutal honesty and I applaud her for that. I know you will, too.

Christine wrote every world of this book from her heart. She wrote it through immense pain and she wrote it with unlimited love. It has helped her overcome the worst loss any mother could suffer and it has helped make her a stronger, wiser and more caring person. This book has already fulfilled its original purpose and now it's time for it to complete it's most important task. I'm sure it will do just that.

Terry Doe

THANK YOU ALL

There are so many wonderful people I need to thank for helping me with this book, if I thanked them all individually I'd need another book to do it. Knowing me, no matter how hard I tried to remember, I'd still forget to thank somebody, so I'd like to do this in a way that includes everyone.

So, my heartfelt love and gratitude goes out to all my lovely family and friends, not only for helping with the book itself, but for everything you did to make sure I was still here to write it. I'll thank one person by name, my darling Alfie, for holding me, and our family, together during those dark, dark days, and for his constant encouragement to keep going with this book, when I really thought I could do no more. Please believe me; I know how lucky I am to have so many good people in my life, and you know I'll never forget what you did for me when I needed it most.

Thank you all. You have my appreciation and my love, forever..

Christine Ball

Me and my Grandson Naylor.
It's times like this that you know
you're never alone.

REMEMBRANCE

It's been thirteen long years since my life changed forever. Some thought I would never make it, and neither did I, for sure. When you hit the lowest point in your life and your world is shattered in a matter of seconds, you feel that no one on this earth could ever feel the pain and heartache like you are going through.

It is days like today, though, as a voice disturbs me from my deepest thoughts and asks, "Are you okay?" when I know that my life is worth living. I glance up and look at a handsome young man, who is driving. He has such a striking resemblance to another young man whom I had once sat beside and loved very much. It's my grandson,

Naylor, who is driving me today, and he looks at me, and smiles with the same shy smile as his dad. It's uncanny how much he resembles my beautiful son, Naylor - even his voice and his laughter. If I close my eyes, sometimes it can make my hair stand up on the back of my neck. My heart feels like it could burst with pride and love for him, knowing how he has grown from a little boy who seemed so lost after losing his dad, and leaving his home to come and live with me and his granddad. At that time, he was feeling as messed up as me, and I'm looking at him today as a beautiful, strong, well-mannered young man, with so much going for him in life. This is what makes me want to live again. The poison that once ran through my veins is long gone; I am no longer lost, and I make the best of every day, along with my husband my beautiful daughter, Phyllis, my son, Alfie, and all my other grandchildren.

It's a special day, today. It's my son, Naylor's birthday so my grandson and I are on our way to the cemetery to take flowers and meet the rest of the family. Today is a bit different, though, because instead of sitting at my son's graveside all day, I decided to go somewhere that has always held a piece of my heart. Over the last 12 years, I have spent hours deep in thought with it on my mind; it's a war memorial for the soldiers who never returned home. Me, my grandson, Naylor, and our good friend, Terry Doe, went along. It was a place that I wanted my grandson to visit as well.

As we pulled our car into the car park, I felt a thud in my heart, knowing that I was about to witness the loss of so many other mothers' sons. I watched as Naylor carried a tribute of white roses that I'd brought to lay in remembrance of all the courageous young men and women, and it's times like this that you know that you were never alone in your deepest time of grief and pain. I walked toward the entrance, and my heart was beating so fast. I felt an overwhelming love for every other mother who had lost their child, and my heart was broken for all those who didn't return home.

I walked around looking at the hundreds of names on the walls, of all the brave young men and women who gave their lives for us so that we could be strong and free, and it made me feel that I had no right to dwell in self-pity for my own loss. As I looked around at all

XII

those names, it put my own life into perspective. How serene it felt to share their glory, and the power that they have left on this earth for us. I felt so strong walking around reading the names of all the loved ones who had sacrificed their lives for us and given us freedom. This is a place I will hold close in my heart, and one that I will visit when feeling low; it truly inspires the weakest mind to go forward and be strong, and it serves a lesson, even in grief, of a cherished loved one. You may suffer pain, but don't give up on your loved one's, family or friends, or your own life. I laid a tribute of white roses and said a silent prayer.

Every day is a blessing to me now, and my heart goes on. I want to live, and as my son, Naylor once said to me a week before I lost him, "Live everyday like it's your last". That's what I try to do - to make every day of my life count. As I've said in the book, my husband and I are rich - not in money, but with our beautiful children and grandchildren, and life itself.

XIII

CHAPTER ONE

TIME STOOD STILL

It was Friday the eighth of August and my husband, Alfie, and I were up early that morning. It was so warm the sun was bright and we were sitting, drinking a cup of tea. I was in a bit of a rush because I had to pick my mum up from her house. She was suffering from cancer so I was taking her to hospital for treatment, and I felt better knowing it was nearly completed, but I was still waiting for my Naylor to call me.

Naylor is my middle son. I have three children; Alfie is the eldest, Phyllis is my only girl, and although Naylor was married with two young sons he always called in every day to see me to have a cup of tea and something to eat. I didn't want to keep my mum waiting so I left home as planned and thought I would phone him later - I knew he would call in on his way home.

I picked up my mum, but we had only got a few miles up the road when the phone rang. I said to my mum: "That will be Naylor, so I put the phone on loudspeaker. "Where are you at, my old gel," he asked me. "I'm taking Nan to the hospital for her treatment," I told him.

Naylor always called in for a cup of tea with his 'old gel'.

"I won't call in if you're not at home," he said. "I'll be-round later." My mum joined in the conversation. "Morning, Nay. How are you?" He told her he was fine but he was more interested in how she was feeling. I could hear in his voice that he was worried about her. He told his nan that he had a present for her. Mum's voice was full of excitement; she was like a child.

"What is it Nay?" she said. "Tell me, what is it?" He was laughing.

"That cheered you up",he said, and then told her that he had a brooch for her. He told her it had different coloured stones in it. Mum said, "thank you" and he told her not to worry about her treatment, that she would be fine. He told her he would call in on the way home to see her and bring her the brooch. He told me he would see me later and then said "luv ur" and I said "luv ur" back. He never said goodbye on any phone calls to me.

After Mum's hospital appointment, we had lunch. Mum was feeling tired so I took her home, and my sister and I got her into bed for a sleep. My husband and I had to go shopping that afternoon because we had a family wedding the next day, and I rang Naylor while I was out and we had a chat, as we did every day.

We carried on shopping and everything was going well. My phone rang and I knew it was Naylor before I looked at it. As I answered I heard him say, "What are you doing, my old gel?" I told him I'd had a long day but it wouldn't be long before we finished our shopping. I asked him what he was up to and he told me he was on his way home and that he would only be about an hour. We chatted for awhile, he told me he would see me later then said, "luv ur" and I said, "uv ur" back, and we hung up. My husband and I had one more stop to make, at Shepherds Bush market. I remember how crowded it was on the streets, but we managed to park. As we were walking around, I stopped and was looking on a stall when I heard Alfie's phone ring. I carried on looking and I heard Alfie speaking. His voice got louder and as I turned round and looked at him, I could see that his face was drained. My heart felt like it was going to stop as I heard the panic in his voice. The only words I could make out were, "It's Naylor! We have got to go. He is hurt!" I was crying and telling Alfie that he can't be. I was on the phone just a short while ago. We both started pushing our way through the crowd.

Romany roots. My Grandad and Granny.

CHAPTER TWO

MY FAMILY BACKGROUND

I come from a Romany family. My mum and dad had four children; there was my elder brother, then me, my sister and our younger brother. The old Romany fathers had good old fashioned values on family life and we were brought up to respect our parents and our elders. The man was always the head of the family, and in a way, it was like a Mafia family. If there was a problem, the father would sort it out and the family would look on him for help. It didn't matter how old you were. You could always rely on him. He would teach his sons all that he knew, and when they married, they became the head of their own families, but the old fathers were the ones we all relied on, until they passed away.

When watching television documentaries of Romany people, some of them are not true when they say that Romany women do not work. I can tell you, my mother worked all her life, along with a lot of other women. Some programmes betray our true Romany culture. We didn't have much money back then. My parents worked alongside each other and my dad worked hard doing what he could to look after us. We travelled in different seasons of the year for work and my mum worked hard, as well as looking after her children.

As we became of school age, they settled so we could all have an education. My dad started to buy and breed horses and that was a wonderful time in my life, helping him to look after them. Although I was only young, if any of the horses was lame or sick I would take care of them. If the vet was brought in, I remember

I loved to look after the horses.

watching and helping and taking in everything he did. The knowledge I learned from him stayed with me throughout the years to come, and was passed on to two generations of children.

Growing up, I remember telling my dad and mum that I wanted to be a vet, but being a girl in a Romany family at that time, it would not be allowed. My role in life was to help look after the family and to learn, from an early age, how to take care of a family of my own one day, although me and my older brother, Lenny, and our cousin, Andrew, had some good times riding the horses bareback through the fields.

My dad's parents both died at the age of 42, leaving him alone with two sisters who he loved very much. My dad was only 18 at that time. His elder sister was married and lived in Bournemouth, and his younger sister joined her, leaving him alone. He travelled about with his uncle from his mum's side of the family.

He told us tales of his mum and dad and always talked about how much he missed them. He made sure that we knew everything about them. I can remember my dad telling us that after he lost his mum and dad so young, even though he was close to his two sisters and would visit them when he could, and they both loved him so much, he always felt very lonely. We looked through some old photos one day, and there's one that always sticks in my mind; it was of my dad sitting in the front seat of a hearse at his dad's funeral. He looked so sad. I asked Dad about that day and he told me that he felt like he was walking under a cloud, and all his sunshine had been taken away. Losing both his parents so young must have torn his world apart, so when he had his own family he appreciated and loved us all very much and gave us all that he'd missed in family life.

My dad looked so sad.
All of his sunshine had been taken away.

CHAPTER THREE

EVERY OCCASION WAS SPECIAL

Every occasion was special to my dad and he loved Christmas. We were brought up to know that it was never about gifts at Christmas time, it was being together as a family and understanding the proper meaning. He and my mum would make so much out of so little. We were always excited when it was time to put our Christmas tree up. It would sparkle with decorations and lights and on Christmas Eve, Mum would start the cooking. She was very old-fashioned in her Romany ways and so was her cooking, which was a delight to eat.

For some reason, I remember Dad always sorting out the fruit. He would get a box and cover it with paper or tinfoil, fill the bottom with paper and mound the fruit up as high as he could, then he would sit it next to the tree. The room looked magical. On Christmas morning, we would be up early, so excited to have a stocking each filled with a few sweets, more fruit, and a small gift each. That's how Christmas was for us, all about being a family and remembering the ones who had died before us.

When Good Friday came, we were never allowed to eat meat. Dad would always go out early that morning and bring home fresh fish and hot cross buns, and Mum would cook our meal. Mother's Day was always a special day, too. We didn't have a car when we were little, but Dad had a lorry that he used for work. I can remember him putting us up in the cab and taking us to the old nursery, and buying Mum daffodils for Mother's Day, until we were old enough to get our own. We never forgot Dad on Father's Day, either. He was a gentleman and everyone that knew him would say so.

On the other hand, there was my mum's family. She had seven brothers and four sisters. Her youngest sister died at the age of eight months, and she also lost a young brother of 23 years old. My mum lost her dad when I was about two, and Mum would tell me stories of how he helped her to look after me. When she had work to do, he would tie me on a piece of string next to him whilst he made wooden clothes pegs. He would also knock on her window late at night to make sure that I was all right. I cherish those memories of him. My Granny lived to be 87. She was a wonderful granny and a very educated lady. It seemed that every comer we went around, there were uncles, aunties, and cousins from my mum's family, and she was loved by them all. She had very strong willpower and was a real Character.

Both my parents were brought up in hard times, but once they got married they formed a very strong family bond. As Romany children, my elder brother and I learned early how to work hard and help with family life. I was the eldest daughter, so my main role was to help to take care of my younger sister and brother. My earliest memory was when I was about six; my young sister was taken ill with polio and it was a very difficult time for my parents. She was in hospital for months. The day arrived when we went to bring her home. She'd had a brace fitted on her leg to help her to walk and a nurse helped her to stand. She took a few steps toward our dad and that was the first time that I saw my dad cry. It was a difficult time for my dad and mum to take care of a sick child.

One day, Dad was out at work and Mum was massaging my sister's leg. Then Mum put her in her push-chair and asked me to give her a push, to get her off to sleep. As I walked down the path, I turned around and looked back at my mum. She was sitting on a chair with her head in her hands, crying. I knew from that young age that my mum needed me to help. I remember stroking my sister's beautiful, auburn hair and singing to her until she went off to Sleep.

Our family moved into a house a few years later and it was a luxury for us all. I have

Mum and dad on their wedding day.

lots of good memories of this time in my life and there's a very fond one of me and my elder brother, Lenny. There was a knock on the front door and our mum answered it. She told me and my brother that the man wanted to talk to us so she sat us down and the man opened this big case. As we both looked in, we could see that it was full of sweets. I'm not sure, but I think he was a rep and he asked us to sample the sweets and tell him what we thought of them. We looked at each other with delight because we didn't have a lot of sweets in those days - our parents couldn't afford them. He gave us one sweet at a time, he and our parents watched us eat them, and after every one we ate he asked, "What was that one like?" Our answers were given with chocolate round our mouths and smiles that reached from ear to ear - "Just right!" It's a memory I will never forget. What a treat!

11

Then Mum was expecting my baby brother. I was sent to school every day and I had friends at school, but once I was home I had to learn how to cook, clean and help to take care of the rest of the family. My dad and mum turned the parlour into a bedroom so there was enough room for the newborn. I can remember helping her to sort everything out. When mum went into hospital to

Myself, my Dad and elder brother Lenny. Fond memories.

have her baby, I stayed home from school to help my dad with the family. He would do most of the cooking whilst I did the cleaning and washing and took care of the other children. From the day Mum brought the newborn home, I learned how to help take care of him. I used to stand by his pram, just about tall enough to see over at him, and as soon as he moved I would be there, and watch as my mum fed him and then put him across her knee to wind him. It wasn't long before I was washing, changing, and feeding him myself. I could take care of him just as well as my mum.

When my baby brother started school, I would take him and then go to school myself. Before we set off, Mum would always say, "Make sure you don't let his hand go until you are at the school gates, and make sure you watch him go in."

One particular day, we were walking along a stretch of road and he was pulling his hand from mine, because he was making out to be an

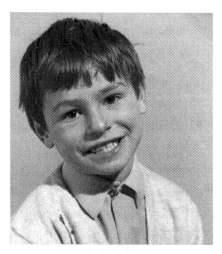

My baby brother Dean.

12

aeroplane so he needed both hands - one out each side of himself. I must have walked on a bit faster, and my brother was just behind me when I heard a cry. I looked back and he was gone. He had fallen in the ditch and it was a long way down. I fell to my knees, reached down and pulled him out and he was covered in mud. I was horrified. I was checking he was all right, wiping the mud off his clothes and he just stood there, startled.

We carried on and went to school, but that taught me a valuable lesson in life. My mum did not repeat herself every morning for nothing. It was to teach me. She was older and wiser and knew how things could happen, so to let me walk my brother to school she must have really trusted me. I always listened to her, but after that I made sure that she could trust me and did exactly as I was told.

That's how the old Romany families brought their children up, on trust. A lot of Romany women worked and that's how families survived, trusting their older children to take care of the younger ones. This is only a glimpse into my life, and how I was brought up, but it was never a chore to help with work, or take care of my brothers and sister. It was a way of life, and I am so proud to be the daughter of that old Romany couple.

CHAPTER FOUR

MARRIED WITH CHILDREN

I met my husband when we were in our teens. He was my elder brother's friend and the first time I saw him we fell in love, and he became my soulmate as well as my husband. Our families lived in the same road and our parents knew each other. My husband had three sisters and two brothers, and it wasn't long before he asked for me - that meant we were going out - and we were engaged and married soon after.

It wasn't hard for me to get on with family life because I was used to running a home and taking care of others, and I missed my own family very much, but as we only lived down the road I saw them most days. My husband had a good family and they became like my own. His elder sister, Pauline, and I were very close in age so we became best friends and have remained so throughout many years.

My husband, Alfie, and I were both over the moon when I became pregnant with our first child, and our parents were overwhelmed because it was the first grandchild on both sides of our families. All the time I was expecting my baby I was fine, but when it was time to give birth there was a bit of panic. I focused on the thought that once the baby was here, it would be no different to when I was at home; I knew everything I

Me and my sister-in-law Pauline. Friends through out the years.

needed to know. How wrong I was! The first time that I held my tiny baby boy, I felt an overwhelming love from deep in my heart. I had never felt like this before and he became my life, from that moment.

The day we took our baby, Alfie, home, as I was laying him in his cot, my husband said in a nervous voice, "Be careful of his head." I looked at him and said, "Don't worry. I know what I'm doing," but I could feel my body shaking. I thought I would calm down after we all got settled, but I didn't; things only got worse. I couldn't sleep because I was checking the baby all night and I put his cot close to my bed so I could hold his hand, and every time I dozed off, I would wake startled and softly nudge the baby to make sure he was still breathing.

I carried on being over-protective and put it down to being a new mum, but it wasn't because it was the same after I had my second beautiful baby boy, Naylor. I know every mother loves their children, but I'd been brought up from a small child to take care of babies and to help with family life. That's part of our Romany culture and it made my taking care of my two little boys more intense. Then I had my third baby, my beautiful little girl, Phyllis Anne; she is our princess and she made our family complete.

My love was unconditional for my children. They became my sun, my moon, my stars. They were the air I breathed and sometimes I knew I was being over-protective, but they were my life. I clearly remember being humiliated one day when my two boys were in their first school.

My three children. My Sun, my Moon, My Stars.

They used to have swimming lessons, and they brought a note home asking them to bring a plastic bag to put their wet swimwear in. I put one in each time they had a lesson, but I would put my finger through it a few times to make holes. One day, I was asked if the head teacher could have a word so I went to her office and she said, "Mrs. Ball, haven't you any bags without holes in?" I had to explain that I put the holes in myself because I was worried in case my boys might play around and put the bags over their heads and suffocate. She laughed. "Oh, Mrs. Ball, don't be silly. Everyone thought you couldn't afford them." I asked who was everyone? She said it had been her, a couple of the teachers, and a few of the Mums.

It became a joke in the school and in our family for years, but no one realised how passionate I was about taking care of my children. I had been taught from so young to spot things that could put a child in danger, and yes, I was a nervous mother in every step of

Christmas was always special.

my children's lives. My role as a mother was to love, take care and protect my children. I have a beautiful family and they all enjoyed a wonderful childhood, especially at Christmas time, that was always special. I loved Christmas and made sure that they did, too. We'd all go out together on family outings and we always made a special occasion of New Year's Eve.

We had our teething problems with our two sons in their teenage years, but no different to any other family with teenage boys, and when there were any problems Alfie and I were always there to help sort it out. All three of our children got married. Alfie and I were very happy and we were still young enough to enjoy life with them when they became parents. We became very young grandparents and our grandchildren were all so beautiful. I was as worried over my grandchildren as I was my own. They were always in and out of our house with their kids. We had a conservatory on the back of our house and it would be full of laughter and noise, especially when they all turned up together. There would be babies crying, children playing and I would be making cups of tea and food.

I remember one day when they were all in the back room, laughing and joking. Alfie and Phyllis were tormenting Naylor about how he always said, 'my mum', and they used to call him 'Mum's pet'. He would get up, put his arms around me and give me a kiss and say, "She is mine. She's my old gel". For some reason, Naylor always needed a bit more reassurance in doing things than my other two

So young as a grandmother with my grandson Alfie.

children and I always did my best to let him know I was there for him, and he trusted me. My other children always joked with him, but he was proud to be very close to his mum. Those days are my treasured memories; the house bursting at the seams with love and happiness.

I was very close to my dad and he had not been well for a long time. When he died suddenly, I was devastated and so was the rest of the family. He was our backbone. The days when I felt really bad, I would think back on how my dad coped when he lost both his parents, and how he looked after us and made his life around his children. It made me stronger and I made sure that I was strong for my children, just like my dad. I lived for my children. I put them first in everything I did, and I was very happy to do so. My mum became ill a few years later. She was diagnosed with cancer and we were all very shocked, but pulled together as a family and looked after her.

All my children were very happy. Alfie and I were at a stage in our lives where our children were settled with their partners, and there was no more waiting up at night for them to come in, or going to parties. We were at the best time of our lives; we were not rich in money, but we were rich in having our children and grandchildren around us. We had taken many paths and some were right, some wrong, but we were at a time of contentment. Looking back, nothing - not even the death of my father who I loved very much - could prepare me for what was about to tear my world apart, piece by piece, and to destroy all I believed in, and put me into darkness.

We were at a time of contentment.

19

My darling son Naylor.

CHAPTER FIVE

THE DESCENT

As we fought our way through the crowd, I remember saying, "Alfie, there must be a mistake. Naylor rang me a short while ago." We got to the car and I was screaming and crying. I knew there was something wrong with Naylor, but couldn't imagine what had happened. Alfie was trying to get out of the traffic and it was like everything was at a standstill. He was still trying to ring around to find out what had happened.

We finally got on the motorway, heading toward Oxford, and Alfie was still talking on the phone. I can remember just rocking with my head in my hands, feeling sick and begging him to get me to my boy.

Naylor was out with one of his mates, Fred, and there had been an accident. Fred was hurt, but not as badly as Naylor. I didn't know if Fred had rung his dad or got someone to ring for him, but it was Fred's dad who was ringing Alfie. I don't know what he told him, Alfie didn't tell me, but it looked bad.

We were driving along for what seemed like ages and then Alfie had another phone call. It was the police who told Alfie that we were going the wrong way, so we turned around to head to where the accident was, but the policeman told us go straight to the hospital. He told us that because it was a country road, the traffic was tailed back for several miles and it would be quicker if we headed straight to the John Radcliffe hospital.

At some time, I must have spoken to a policeman on the phone, because I can remember asking him if Naylor was all right. He told me that it had been a bad accident, but to try not to panic too much whilst we were driving. He said everything possible was being done and that there was an air ambulance on its way for my Naylor. As soon as he said that, I thought, "Please God, help him. There must be hope or they wouldn't have got the air ambulance. He's got to be all right. They've got an air ambulance for him." I was holding my hands together, praying for Naylor to hold on. In my heart, I believed I was holding his hand and I was begging him to hold on until I could get to him and help him.

Looking back, I don't know how Alfie drove the car because I was hysterical, and he was crying. Then, suddenly, it was like someone had hit me with a stun gun. I looked at Alfie and said, "Our boy's gone." I will never know why I said that, it was just a feeling I had, and as quickly as it came, it went.

Then I started repeating myself and saying, "Stay with me Nay. Don't leave me." It seemed to take forever on the road and then the phone rang again. I don't know how I got talking to the policeman, but I remember asking him if he could tell me what was happening. I asked if Naylor was on his way to hospital and he told me that Fred had been taken in the air ambulance, not Naylor. To be honest, from my heart I knew it was too late for my baby, but I remember just willing Naylor to live. I could not give up. He was my baby and out of my three children, he was the one who depended on me the most. I couldn't let go. This was the time in his life when he needed me the most and I knew if he could talk he would be asking for his mum. All I wanted to do was to hold him and tell him I was there.

We finally got to the hospital but we must have taken the wrong entrance because we were at the back of the building. I was still crying and I heard Alfie asking someone where Accident and Emergency was, and we ran through corridors as fast as we could until we got to the front desk. Alfie was talking, but I was still hysterical and I heard him giving Naylor's name. The receptionist told him that no one had been brought in yet by that name and we'd best wait, so we stood by the front doors so that we wouldn't miss him when they arrived. It seemed that we waited for hours, and to be honest, I still don't know how long we waited. I think there must have been family there by then, but the only one I can remember was my brother-in-law, Tony. Everything else seems very vague; all I was doing was running to every ambulance as it pulled up, expecting my Naylor to be sitting in one.Even though I had this terrible feeling inside, I couldn't give up on my baby. By this time, I think Fred had been taken to a different hospital.

At one point, Alfie told me that he'd spoken to someone, and said it didn't look good. I didn't want to know. I just wanted Naylor. I recall my eldest son, Alfie, being there, and my daughter Phyllis and her husband, Billy; my daughter-in-law, Rosy, was there and Naylor's wife Sue. I remember a policeman being there as well, but all I knew was that I was being taken to Naylor. I know I was walking with them and that I looked down and didn't have any shoes on. I don't know until this day what happened to them.

The policeman was talking to me but I can't remember what he said. I think it was my son, Alfie, who said he was taking me to Naylor. I will never forget walking through a door and there lay my beautiful boy. It looked just like he was asleep and I must have lost it because I was crying, telling him to wake up, and as I was kissing him on his face, I saw that his eyes were not quite closed. I know he would have been looking for me and I was telling him, "I am here, Nay. Your mum's here. Please wake up. Don't leave me."

The room was full of our family and I told them I wanted to be on my own. I don't know if they all went out. I just wanted to pick up my baby's head from the pillow and hold him. I could only see a blue mark around the side of his mouth, and I think I was told not to move him, but what mother would not have done what I did? I put my hand gently under his poor head and tried to cradle him to me and I remember barely lifting his head and softly kissing his forehead. I was frightened I was going to hurt him. As I held him, it felt as if my hand was wet and as I took my hand away slowly, there was my baby's blood on it. I was sobbing and that moment will stay with me for the rest of my life.

I knew my Naylor was hurt so badly, and here was I, his mum, the one who should have been able to help him, to take care of him, protect him, and my heart was smashed into a thousand bits. How could I, his mother, have let this happen to him? I'd told him as a little boy, and all through growing up, that I would always be there when he needed me. It was all I knew, to look after my children, and here lay my beautiful Naylor. At the time, he needed me the most, I couldn't get to him. In my heart, I felt that I failed him as a mother. I can remember my father-in-law giving me a tablet, and I think it was to calm me down, but I don't know how Alfie got me out. It didn't feel real, but I know we were in the car with my elder brother, Lenny, and his wife, Linda. I can't recall what was said or much about the journey home.

My son, Alfie, lived next door to us and there was family in and out of both houses. Alfie and I sat on the settee holding hands and crying all night. For the first time, when our boy needed us the most in his life, we were helpless. They say that when trouble comes calling, there is no warning, and our lives were shattered in the blink of an eye, and our Naylor was taken away. Because the accident happened late afternoon and my mum had been to hospital that day and she was ill at the time, my brothers didn't tell her until early next morning. When they brought her to me, she walked into the room, a tall, slim woman who had been strong all her life and she sat down with me and Alfie, her poor eyes red where she'd been crying. Her first instinct was to take care of me and she just kept repeating herself, saying to

Alfie and me, "Why couldn't it be me and not my beautiful Naylor? I'm ill and old and I've got cancer. Why couldn't it have been me?"

My niece, who had been with my mum that afternoon, and looking after her, told us later that every time the phone rang that evening, Mum shouted from her bedroom, "That will be my Naylor. He's calling in to see me. He told me he's got me a lovely brooch, and he's probably running late." She didn't know it was my brothers checking that no one would tell her what had happened until they were with her. She waited for Naylor until she fell asleep.

A lot of family and friends arrived early that morning. The house was full of people paying their respects, but I can't remember who they were. People were talking to me but it was like I wasn't there; my thoughts were with Naylor. I remember this sick feeling in my stomach and I had tight pains in my chest. I just kept asking Alfie to take me to my baby. Alfie told me that he was taking me, but he said he didn't know if we would be able to see him. I didn't care, as long as I was there.

He decided we would go alone. Being of Romany culture, the first thing family and friends wanted to do was be with us. They didn't feel we should be on our own because we always stick together, especially at times like this. Most times, Romanies turn up in crowds and straight away people tar us all with the same brush and feel under threat. Our family knew that, but they knew how much I wanted to be with Naylor so we went on our own.

We didn't speak much in the car. We were crying and couldn't believe what we were doing on our way to a mortuary to see our son. It felt like I'd had a bad dream. This was not true. How could my boy be gone? How could he be taken like this? I was so mixed up. As we got on the motorway I can remember saying to Alfie, "Smash into the barrier and kill us both because we're finished." How could we live without our boy? As I looked at him begging him to kill us, I will never forget the look on his face. He said, "What about our other children?" At that time, though, I couldn't see anybody but Naylor. Tears were running down Alfie's face and I will never understand how my poor husband drove us to the hospital. We must have brought flowers - I can't remember where.

As we arrived at the hospital, I felt sick and faint. We pulled in front of the mortuary and Alfie got out and rang the bell, but no one answered. Alfie said it was because it was Saturday and I was devastated. I could only think that my beautiful young man was in there, hurt and all alone. I was hysterical and crying to Alfie to help me to be with him, but he was as helpless as I was.

There was a gate on the side of the building and as I ran toward it I saw a back door. I knew my baby was in there so I squeezed through a gap and banged on it. By this time, Alfie was trying to pull me away, saying, "We shouldn't be here." All the time, I just keep begging him to help me, telling him that Naylor knew I was there, and I just wanted to tell him I loved him. He let go of me and I laid my body up against the wall of the mortuary as Alfie went back toward the gate, crying.

I carried on talking to Naylor, telling him I was sorry that the day he needed me the most in his life he was so far away and I couldn't get to him. I had never known such a feeling that took over my body. It felt like I was drowning in pain, and I had this picture in my head from the night before, when I put my hand under his head and how badly my beautiful boy was hurt. It was unbearable knowing that he was just behind the wall I was lying against. I remember calling out for Naylor, my legs were like jelly and my body was trembling with fear. Alfie came to me and said we had to leave from there, and we were hanging on to each other, crying for our boy. We went back to the car.

Alfie sat me in the car and told me to try to rest my head, and as he was talking to me, a car pulled up and a woman got out. She walked toward the office and as she opened the door Alfie walked to her and said, "We came to be with Naylor." The woman explained that she couldn't let us in and we asked time and time again but she still refused. I didn't understand why she wouldn't let us in and then she told us that there had been a really bad accident on the motorway. Two families had been killed and they were being brought in. We gave her the flowers we had brought and asked if they could be put with Naylor. She promised us that they would.

We sat back in the car. We just wanted to stay near for as long as we could, and after a while we saw two private ambulances turn up, one behind the other. They were let through the same gate that I had squeezed through and although Alfie and I were in a terrible state of grief and pain, it was a sadness that will always stay with me, knowing two families had set out on a journey, never to return. We drove away and I can't remember speaking on the way home. I was hurting so bad, knowing that we had left our baby on his own. I was getting flashbacks of the night before and just keep going back over Naylor's life, remembering when he was a little boy and how I told him I would always protect him and be there when he needed me.

I remember thinking back to a day when Nay and I were out in my backyard. I was tidying up and he was cleaning his dogs out and I cut my finger on a piece of wood and cried out to him. He dropped what he was doing and ran to me, quickly took my hand and ran it under the outside tap, then wiped it with the bottom of his shirt and said, "It's all right, my old gel. It's only a small cut." He kissed my hand I will never forget that day, and how he showed his love for his mum.

My Naylor.
Memories flow back to when he was a little boy.

My head was filled with so many emotions, and all I wanted to do was to die and be with my baby. In my head, all I could hear was him calling me and I felt numb. We got home and there were loads of family and friends all come to mourn our boy and show their respects to the family. That's the true culture of proper Romanies. We stand by each other in times like this. Although I was in shock, and I can't remember who was there at the time, over the years my family have told me there were so many, and I thank each and every one of them for being with us in our deepest hours of need.

CHAPTER SIX

SITTING UP

Sitting up has been a tradition that Romanies have followed for centuries when someone passes away. Almost as quickly as turning on a light-switch, friends and family will come from all over the country to show their respects, and try to do anything to help the family. I mentioned earlier that Romany families are like the Mafia. When a family is in troubled times and needs help, we stick together and that's one of the values that I love about my culture. My son, Alfie, lived next door to us so both houses and gardens were being used for people to sit up. Mourners would come and go, and some of our family moved in and stayed. I couldn't eat, and I can't remember talking much. My sister has told me since that I just sat, rocking, with a picture of Naylor clutched to my chest.

In the meantime, Alfie and both our families were sorting out arrangements. Alfie walked into the room trying to tell me that he had sorted out bits of the funeral and that he'd ordered so many black cars. I know I had been taking tablets to keep me calm, but when I heard him mention black cars, something flashed into my mind about a conversation that Naylor and I'd had one day at a close family funeral.

It's an old tradition in a cortege of cars, even though the family nearly always book too many, that none of them remain empty. At this particular funeral, Naylor, his wife, and I were standing together and Naylor just spoke out the blue and said he didn't like the black cars, and I said, "You must have read my mind. I was just thinking the same thing." He told me he was pleased that he'd brought his own car and told me that if anything happened to him, he didn't want black cars. I told him that's how I felt. I didn't want black cars when I died, either. I think this stemmed from the sad loss of my dad. Naylor told me he didn't like travelling in them and as we were talking, my cousin walked over and asked if we would fill the last car. Without hesitation, Naylor told me to go with his dad and he walked toward the car with his wife and got in, and as the car drove by me, I thought how much he resembled my dad. After the funeral, I told him that I would have got in the car, but he told me I didn't have to and that he had done it for me. He also told me that he didn't want to get in another one, and he never did.

I never discussed what we spoke about with anyone else. I must have put it to the back of my mind until Alfie walked in the room and I told him I didn't want black cars for Naylor. I don't think Alfie knew what I was on about until I told him that Naylor hated the black cars, and when I told him of the conversation that Naylor and I'd had, he cancelled the cars straight away. I said how much Naylor loved horses and I wanted white cars - I didn't care what they were, as long as they were white.

The days turned into nights and more and more people came to mourn our son. The day came when my baby was coming home from

John Radcliffe, Oxford, back to the chapel of rest at Slough. Memories are very vague, but for some reason some stay with me very strong and clear, like that day. We didn't want Naylor to come all that way back on his own, so although there were arrangements already made, we went along with some of our family to follow Naylor back.

Once we got there, and before we started our journey, I think it was me that wanted to see Naylor, but I can't remember seeing him. My mind seems to have blanked out that part of the day. I can remember crying and telling Alfie that I didn't want my Naylor to be on his own, so he asked the driver if it would be all right for me to ride in the van with our son. First of all, he said they were not allowed and it was not their policy to do so, but all the family begged so much that they let me ride with them.

It was a van that picked Naylor up because, as I said before, he did not like black cars. The family have told me since that the two young men who were driving the van looked very worried because they had not allowed this before, and looking back, I can understand why. I was drugged on tablets, going crazy with grief and crying that I didn't want my baby to be on his own.

I remember the family telling me to calm down. One of the young men helped me into the van and they sat me in the middle of them. I told them I would never forget what they had done that day, and I can honestly say I never will. It meant so much to be with my Naylor on that long journey home.

I remember thinking, 'Dear God! What am I doing taking my baby home in a box?' I felt faint and sick to my stomach. The sweat was running down my back and I kept talking to Naylor in my mind, telling him that his mum was with him, and that I loved him so much. The young men were talking to me and asking me if I was all right. My mind was all over the place. How could my Naylor have walked out of his front door that morning, never to return? The last time I had spoken to him and the last time I'd seen him was running through my head and I felt worthless as a mother not being able to do anything to help him.

It was a long journey and I asked the two young men to promise me that they wouldn't let anyone hurt my baby anymore. I told them he was hurt enough and I just wished I could turn back the hands of time. I remember coming into familiar surroundings and pulling into a long drive. The van stopped, the young man opened the door and he helped me out. Alfie and my family were behind him and I was crying because I knew that I had to leave my baby again My clothes felt wet. I remember the sweat was running off me with fright and fear and Alfie told me to try to keep calm. He said that the lady who owned the funeral directors, who was called Pat, had said we could see Naylor. There were quite a few of our family with us as we waited for a while, and then Alfie said we could go in. Alfie and my brother were holding me and the only thing I can remember is walking toward a door and that's it - Alfie told me I had passed out.

When I came round, I can remember crying for Naylor and they calmed me down and said they were taking me to see him, but Alfie told me that as soon as we got near Naylor I blacked straight out again.

Over the next few days, my family took me back several times to see Naylor at the chapel of rest, but every time, I passed out. My sister told me I was so bad on one visit to the chapel, that Pat thought I had died and she had a bad asthma attack herself. I was told that Pat had become very worried about me and I can't remember seeing Naylor at the chapel of rest.

One night whilst we were still sitting up, some of my family were in the front room with me and the only way I can explain how I felt when they were talking is that it was like being underwater. I would be sitting, staring at them and their mouths would open and shut, and I would probably catch the last word they said. I had so many people around me, but I felt lonely and hurt. I was dying inside and all I could hear was Naylor's voice in my head, telling me he needed me. All I wanted was my baby back and I was drowning in pain. My heart was torn out and I was screaming inside. I wanted to die to be with him and I looked around the room thinking, "You have all got each other; he's on his own."

I am ashamed to say now that I didn't see how much my other boy, Alfie, and my beautiful young girl, Phyllis, needed their mum when they had lost their brother, who they loved. From as early as sitting up, I can remember thinking, 'how could my husband, Alfie, watch this destroy our lives?'

We were sitting up one evening and one of my family said, "There's someone come to see you," and as I looked up I saw a young man. He sat down beside me and held my hand; it was one of Naylor's best mates, Paul Vassy, and his wife, Jo. Naylor always called him Bassy. Bassy spoke of how he and Naylor were talking on the phone just before the accident happened, and I can remember him taking off his glasses and wiping the tears from his eyes. He was so distraught and that memory sticks in my mind. Even though I was in so much pain and grief myself, this young man had given me comfort, knowing how much he cared for my son and what a good friend he had been to my Naylor.

Many of Naylor's friends came to see me and show their respect, and from my heart I thank every one of them. I caught the end of someone's conversation about Naylor's clothes being brought home, and I began to scream and asked why they hadn't been brought to me. The next thing I remember was being in hospital. I was lying on a bed and there was an ambulance driver telling me to listen to him and calm down. He was half lying on the bed and holding my hands. My sister said I was telling him that Naylor was hurt so badly and I couldn't get to him. I told him Naylor would have been asking for me. He told me that his being here was more than a coincidence. The day of the accident, he was working on the phone line giving out instructions to people who were in accidents and needing help. He told me he had given instructions to a young lady who was giving Naylor resuscitation. He remembered his name and he told me that the girl had followed his instructions, but it was too late. Naylor had died instantly.

I remember the family asking how this could be coincidence? It was Naylor's way of letting his mum know he was with her, for the same person who was trying to save his life that day was with me this night. At this time in my life now, I know it was our bond; it was strong and it couldn't be broken. I know I asked the doctors to give me something to put me to sleep. I would have done anything to get away from the place I was in. When we came home from the hospital, they gave me Naylor's clothes and I held his T-shirt which still had his blood on it. I felt traumatised and cuddled them into my chest and kept asking for this nightmare to go away. Romany families always bring their loved ones home for the funeral. It could be for a week, or it may be one night and I asked Alfie to bring Naylor home for as long as we could, but he said it was going to be for two nights.

The night before our Naylor was corning home, air-conditioning machines were brought in because it was August and the temperature was soaring. Looking back now, the room was full of my memories, which were of love and happiness and it was where I was waiting for my beautiful boy to come home.

The front room had been got ready for Naylor. The family had brought in a recliner garden chair for me so they could lay it back for me. Alfie was sitting in an arm chair. Alfie told me that the family were all sitting up outside and had left us to be alone in the back room to try to get some rest. By this time, I was taking a lot of tablets. Alfie told me that I was knocked out with the tablets I was taking, and he was resting his head. We were alone when he felt a warm breath on the side of his face, and the feeling of Naylor being with him. Now remembering how drugged I was, within seconds of him feeling this, he said I sat up in the chair and said, "My baby just ran his fingers through my hair." I think we both knew that he came home to us.

The next day, I can remember waiting for Naylor to be brought home. I was taken to the front room where Naylor lay in a casket and all I wanted to do was be with him. He looked so young and handsome and it was like he was sleeping. Once I was with him, I wouldn't leave the room. I held his hand and kissed him on the face telling him his mum was with him.

Every now and then as I was looking at my beautiful son, I thought I could see him breathing and I laid my hand on his chest to feel his heartbeat. The family were in and out the room and we didn't leave him on his own for a second.

34

Down the Splash.

CHAPTER SEVEN

THE FUNERAL

The funeral had been arranged and Alfie knew by now that Naylor hated black cars and we both knew about Naylor's love of horses. He had horses throughout his life. He would drive horses to the local splash to wash them down and swim with them. The horse that took Naylor to his place of rest was one that he used to drive regularly, as a young boy, for a friend of ours, John Finny, so the horse, called Flower, was loaned for the funeral to carry our baby on a London trolley. Kathleen Finny was a good friend of Naylor, and as she said in her memories of him, "It was like old Flower knew what she was doing that day, taking her old friend on that long, last journey together."

I will never know how Alfie held himself together and arranged the funeral. He has since told me that he just wanted to put our son to rest and it was up to him, as the father to do so.

I have only a few vague memories of my Naylor's funeral so I have relied on family and friends to help me put this chapter together. When I think of that morning, I still get a churning feeling in my stomach. My Naylor was home for two days and I felt he was back with us. I never left him and here I was waiting for him to leave me forever. I felt so ill. I had pains in my chest and it felt like I was going to stop breathing, my body was shaking so much.

My sister told me that my two brothers had to hold me up. I can remember my son's two little boys; they wore cream suits with short trousers and, in my heart, I wanted to hold them and protect them from what was happening. If my son had been able to talk to me, I know that's what he would have wanted, but I didn't have the power to hold myself up.

Naylors Son (Naylor) on the day of his dad's Funeral.

I've been told that there were hundreds of family and friends from all over the country, and there were many lorries and trucks carrying floral tributes. Across the road from us was a pub, the Fox and Pheasant, and the landlady, Jenny, closed for the day out of respect, but left the doors of the pub open for people to use the toilets because there were so many of us.

Someone gave Naylor's youngest boy, Razzo a camera. He was only four and he must have just been taking photos randomly. There was one taken in one of the cars and my sister-in-law, Mary Anne, was crying and looked so distraught; he didn't understand what was happening and there were photos of everyone out the front.

My sister-in-law. Mary Anne, distraught.

Alfie's cousin, Billy, and friend, Joe, were walking the horse that was carrying our boy and after the funeral someone told Alfie that they were very distressed and upset. It was so hard for Billy and Joe to take a young boy they both knew so well to his place of rest. I should imagine that it was one of the hardest things they'd had to do, and I will hold them in my heart forever for being there and helping us at such a sad and hard time in our lives.

37

Our eldest son, Alfie, rode on the trolley alongside his much-loved brother with his arm over the casket, and the cortege of white cars, and so many family and friends, and the trucks and lorries that carried the flowers, stretched for miles, I have been told. There are just traces of that day in my mind, but it felt like it was evening, just getting dark. I knew what was happening, but my body was numb and I can't remember being in the cars; it's like an almost complete memory block.

I look at the photos that Razzo took and there's a flash of memory that breaks through and then I wonder where it goes. I remember sitting in the church, but I can't recall coming out of there. Then I remember being under a sort of cover and I now know that it was a gazebo that they had put over Naylor's place of rest.

Support for Naylor's brother Alfie.

The family has told me since that Pat, from the funeral directors, had given the family a bottle of oxygen to carry with them. I think she was worried because I was passing out a lot. My sister told me that they had a wheelchair for me at the graveside, but the only memory I have from the graveside is my daughter smacking me round the face. It must have been when I passed out, and she was trying to tell me to finish what I had to do. I can't remember any more than that.

I have been told that the newspapers were there, but one of the family asked them to leave, because we didn't want to remember that day. I didn't realise when we left the church at Horton that my husband walked behind the horse-drawn trolley carrying our son, and everyone had walked with him. Someone close told me that they had looked behind them as they were walking, and it was like a sea of white shirts.

At the cemetery, there were so many people that it was covered. The family arranged a reception at Iver village hall and I can vaguely remember someone giving me a cup of tea and offering me a sandwich. Alfie said I hadn't eaten since the day of the accident. I know I had this sickness inside from the pain. I would look around at family eating and think, 'how can you eat? I would feel upset when anyone offered me food. I couldn't eat; my baby was gone.

Alfie brought me home and as I was helped into the front room, I only remember how empty I felt and I asked for the tablets that my doctor had prescribed. I was crying for Naylor, and the medication would make me drowsy and I'd sleep for a while, but I would wake in a panic screaming for someone to help me. I can't remember talking to anyone that day.

That evening, all our friends and relatives had gone home and it was our own family left with us. We hadn't slept properly for over two weeks and someone must have suggested that we went to bed to try to get some sleep. I wouldn't leave the settee so my daughter, Phyllis, made a bed on the floor next to me. Everyone was exhausted. As soon as I laid my head down and dozed I would wake up screaming and Alfie tried to calm me. Although I couldn't get to the scene of the accident that day, every time I dozed, I would wake up thinking I was there. I would hold on to anyone who was near me until the fear passed and they would tell me to try to rest. "It's just a nightmare," they said, but I was living in the nightmare.

CHAPTER EIGHT

SHOCK

In the days after the funeral, although I had my other children I felt so lonely and isolated from everybody. Phyllis was staying with us and Alfie lived next door, and close family were taking it in turns to be with us during the day, but night-time was my enemy. I was begging the family not to go to bed. I wanted them to stay up all night. I would lie on the settee, Phyllis would make a bed on the floor for her and her baby, Sonny, next to me, but as soon as I dozed off, I would wake up screaming and crying, shaking with fear with the same nightmare. I wasn't eating, barely drinking and not sleeping properly and the strain was beginning to take its toll on the family.

Every time I had a nightmare it ended in a panic attack and everybody was woken up. I thought I was at the accident, even though I was never there; or it would go from the first time I saw my beautiful boy lying on that bed with his eyes not quite shut and I knew he was looking for me, or knowing how badly he was hurt when I cradled his poor head. He was gone and it was too late. My head felt like it would explode.

I couldn't live without him. How does a mother cope with this? I would ask myself, time after time, and I would pray that I would die so that I could be with him. The attacks got so bad that they must have triggered something in my head and I would pass out. The same thing had happened every time I'd been taken to see Naylor at the chapel of rest. Every day, we would all go to the cemetery and sit there and I always had a numb feeling and when I was spoken to, most times I would look at whoever was talking and probably catch mid-sentence or the last couple of words they had said, and just stare at them. The floral tributes filled one side of the cemetery at that time, and I can't remember that clearly, but a good friend of ours, Terry Doe, took pictures of all the flowers after the funeral, so I know there was something designed in floral to mark everything Naylor had loved in life.

A sea of flower tributes.

Deep inside I had an empty feeling. If I heard a phone ring, for one second my mind would slip and I would think it could be Naylor, but not being able to talk to him or see him, the loss was unbearable. I was in this deep dark place and I couldn't get out, but every now and then I would get a glimpse of a beautiful memory that I shared with Naylor, like the day me and Naylor, and his wife, Sue, where sitting in my backyard watching their boys play. Razzo wasn't very tall for his age and in a month or so he would be starting school. Naylor said he couldn't wait to see him in his little school uniform, and as we were all laughing and joking saying that he didn't look old enough, there was a moment that stands still in my mind; the love that showed in my Naylor's face as he gazed at his two boys, and the proud man he had become of his beautiful family. There was a look of great contentment for his life, and although I have lots of wonderful memories of Naylor, there are a few that I hold dear - like on that day, with just a glimpse as his mum, I captured that photo in my mind and I will hold it in my heart forever.

The saddest thing was, Naylor never got to see his little boy start school. Although I was very ill at the time, on Razzo's first day my husband, Alfie, took me there to meet my daughter-in-law, Sue, to see Razzo start school. I stared as Naylor's two handsome little boys walked toward me, both in their uniforms. I kissed them and gave them a cuddle, and my heart was beating so hard that it felt like it would burst with pain, but also with pride

Razzo's first day at school.

for my son; he wasn't there in person, but he will always be in my heart. What a mixed feeling that was! That was to be the first of many things that Naylor, would miss in his two young sons' lives. Our lives were in turmoil. The family took me to the doctor once again, asking for something to make me sleep and to help stop the nightmares, but no matter what pills I took they still came back, night after night, and even if I dozed in the day, it was the same.

Alfie was distraught with grief himself and he was so worried because I still wasn't eating. My daughter had made him a sandwich and he has since told me that I stared at him and asked, "How can you eat?" This was weeks after the funeral and I still couldn't see how much

43

my two other children needed me. My body would shake with nerves when I saw my Naylor's little boys and my other little grandchildren. All I had known and been brought up to do was to protect and look after my children. I had lost one son and I couldn't be with him, and I couldn't see the others through this thick barrier that had formed around my body. I wanted to reach out to them but was trapped. It was like being in a bubble. My life had been torn apart.

I would look at my husband, Alfie, and think, "Why can't you do something?" Inside, I would be crying and thinking, "You are the man. It's up to you to put things right." Not even my poor mother could help me. She came round every day and cooked, to try to make me eat, even though she was very ill herself, but everywhere I looked at home held a memory of my beautiful young man and I didn't want to eat. I couldn't do anything. I wanted to die. In the early hours of one morning, I had a nightmare and shouted for my daughter, but she was so exhausted from all the stress and dealing with her own grief of losing her brother, she didn't wake. I must have got up, but I don't even remember going out of the door. I had picked up the car keys and driven to be with Naylor. I can't even think how I drove the car. I have one vague memory of that time it was of a beautiful young girl standing over me I thought at the time that I was dying and she was my angel. The family found out later that it had been a young girl visiting her dad's grave early before school and she was worried and tried to wake me. The next thing I knew was my husband and daughter waking me up. I must have fallen asleep on my boy's grave. I don't know how long I was there; the front of the car was in the hedgerow.

That was when my sister had to move in with us, to take it in turns to sit with me so that Phyllis and Alfie could get some rest. I was taken to the doctor again and he told Alfie that it was like I was living in my own world. I was offered to see a psychiatrist, but my husband told the doctor that he and the family were looking after me. A Romany family think it taboo to see a psychiatrist, and taking the chance of being put in a clinic. They would have been failing in their responsibility of taking care of me - especially Alfie, being the man of our Family.

The house was like a bus-stop. People would come, people would go, and this had been going on since the funeral. Even with all the family there, I still felt isolated in a world of my own, looking around myself wondering how everyone was getting on with everyday life. My sisters-in-law had a routine. They would take it in turns coming round each day to help, but I was getting so weak. I still couldn't seem to swallow. I felt sick just looking at food. Whoever was in the kitchen would always make me a cup of tea and a sandwich, and they would put it next to me, but if they didn't pick the cup up and put it to my mouth and make me take a sip, I wouldn't think to touch it.

At this point, I could feel myself fading. I couldn't tell you how I went to the bathroom, or how I washed or dressed. My grandchildren would be in and out the house all day' Phyllis' eldest son, Billy, was four years old and he must have heard the family say I wasn't eating. He would pick up my sandwich, put it to his mouth, take a bit and open and shut his mouth making chewing movements, then put the sandwich to my mouth. I would take the smallest bit and he would smile at me, as if to say, 'I can make her eat, and it wasn't long before all the grandchildren were doing the same.'

When we went to the cemetery, we would sit there for ages. Alfie would always get food for the children and Naylor's eldest son, Naylor, would be eating his chips whilst I sat on the bench. He would take one bit, then walk over to me and put the other half in my mouth. It was like a child feeding a child, although I have been told that, even though by this time I was in a world of my own, if a child cried I would respond and ask why they were crying. By this time, I was just thinking in my own mind that I wanted to die and be with Naylor, I told Alfie every day that I wanted to die and that I needed to be with my baby. The thought of him being on his own was destroying me and these thoughts made my head spin, day after day. I can only describe the feeling as being in a dream, screaming out for help, but no one could hear me.

Some days, when my mum came round and cooked the family a meal, I would take a bit of the children's food now if they offered it, but it was barely a bit. I would never eat a meal. Deep inside I was starving myself and it was like a punishment.

Being a mother was the greatest achievement in my life and I had no regrets about how I loved and brought my children up. It would go round and round in my head; the only thing I was guilty of was not being able to help my baby now, and the only way out was to be with him. I don't know how my family coped. If I dozed off I would be woken by fear of what had happened and I'd grab hold of whoever was next to me and hold them so tightly, screaming until the fear passed.

Alfie knew by now that I meant what I said when I told him I wanted to be with Naylor, because he wouldn't allow me to be on my own. I was taking more pills and I'd started wearing my Naylor's T-shirt - the one he was wearing on the day of the accident. I know Alfie said I should take it off and put it away, but I have been told since that I would cling to it and start crying, and I wore it every night.

I found out later that it had been my daughter who had been bathing me, and my husband would have to help her get me to the bathroom and help her to hold me up so that I didn't fall, the times I couldn't stand. I have been told I would not allow the T-shirt to be washed, so when the nightmares and panic came, the sweat would run down my body like water and the shirt would stick to my back.

There was an imprint of my baby's blood on my back, and they had to wash it off. It must have traumatised them to have to do this, but I didn't know what I was doing. If I'd known I could never have hurt them in this way, and my young daughter, Phyllis, having to take care of all my personal needs - the sort of things I would not let nurses help me with when I had been in hospital to give birth to my babies - as a Romany woman, it would not be in my nature to go into any more detail than that.

My sister, Charmain, had made a plan for me when it was her turn to be with me at night, so that when the nightmares came she was right next to me. She told me not to scream out if I needed her, I was to squeeze her hand to wake her because she knew the rest of the family were all at breaking point, they were so distraught. I did as my sister asked, but I would squeeze her arm so tightly, she told me, her arms were 'mortified'.

I always liked the prayer, 'Footsteps in the Sand', but I could never recite it. My sister told me that during the night I would repeatedly recite the prayer, over and over, and that I knew it word for word. I kept saying, "Where are you Lord, when I need you the most in my life?" If I were asked to recite it now, though, I couldn't tell you unless I read it. I still don't know today how I knew that prayer off by heart.

The family was trying to function the best they could. My daughter had been staying with me since the day of the accident to help look after me, but I was lost in a world of my own. I was traumatised and lying on the settee wrapped in a blanket, the only place I went was to the doctor and the cemetery.

One day, I was really upset and I hadn't slept all night. Every time I closed my eyes I was getting bad flashbacks of the day of the accident and I can only tell you that it was like fireworks going off in my head. Everything was so loud in my head. I remember telling Alfie that I wanted to go to the cemetery to be with Naylor. I was trying to tell him I'd had enough, I couldn't go on anymore, but once we were there, I was crying and shouting, saying there were too many people around me all the time. I told him I wanted to be left alone.

I had bunch of roses to put in a vase and Alfie had bought me a new pair of flower-cutters with thick, stainless blades to cut the thick, woody stems of the roses. We cut the flowers and I was sitting on the bench crying and I said I just needed to be on my own. He said he didn't want to leave me, but I told him I would be fine. After a bit of arguing, he finally agreed and I watched him walk away. I was staring at my son's photo on his grave and my mind was wandering from one memory to another. It was cold by now and I had a thick, black coat on, but I started to sweat and shake and I felt like there was an explosion in my head. I couldn't control the panic and fear. I could hear Naylor calling me and I was telling him that I was going to be with him and look after him. In my mind, I knew what I had to do.

CHAPTER NINE

LIVING THE NIGHTMARE

As I looked down I saw the cutters. Alfie must have forgotten to take them. I picked them up, cut straight into my wrist and the first cut I made, the blood covered my hand. I can't say it was done in a frenzy because it wasn't - just one cut. I made cut after cut; the steel cutters sliced through my skin like paper. I remember talking to Naylor all the time I was doing it and in my head, I could hear him. I had made about a five-inch cut deep across my wrist. Then I started cutting across lower, I even dug the cutters deep so I would cut into a vein, and all the time I was doing this I didn't feel any pain, but after a while I did feel faint and dizzy. I remember looking up and I saw a lady walking toward me. She was carrying a bunch of flowers and she must have been visiting a grave. As she approached closer, I let my arm drop to the side so it could not be seen. I hung my head and turned my legs to hide the blood on the floor. She had passed straight by not noticing what I had done, but by now the sleeve of my coat was soaked with blood.

I went to stand up and to try to lie next to my baby, near his grave. I could hear him calling me so clear and all the time I was telling him, "I know you have been hurt. I'm going to be with you," but I couldn't stand, my legs were like jelly and I slumped back on the bench. My head was hanging down when I noticed the blood on the floor. I felt like I was going to pass out I was ready to die and be with Naylor.

I don't know if my phone had rung or what, but it was in my hand at this point and I could see my younger brother, Dean's name on the screen. I don't know how I got talking to him, but I can remember him asking me how I was. I told him I was fine. He's told me since that he'd said, "Where are you?" and I told him I was with Naylor.

My brother, Dean, had been working not too far away. He thought that I had sounded down but he hadn't realised that I was on my own. He decided to come to the cemetery to see me, and he knew there was a bit of cementing to do on a couple of slabs, so he thought he would bring some cement in a bucket to sort them out. Next thing, I saw my brother walking down the drive of the cemetery.

My head was filled with so many emotions. The only thing I can remember was my brother approaching closer toward me. It looked like everything was in slow motion, and although I was slumped forward I'll never know how I remained on the bench.

He dropped the bucket and started screaming, "Oh no! What have you done?" He was frantic and he grabbed the cutters from my lap and threw them as far as he could; they were never to be found. He took off his jumper and tied it around my upper arm to try to stop the bleeding, and then he pulled me up. The only thing I can remember was being in his truck and going across a roundabout, then being at the hospital.

My brother booked me in and told the nurses what had happened. By now, the rest of the family had turned up at the hospital, my wrist had been stitched and bandaged and I was put in a bed. My daughter, Phyllis, and my sister, Charmain, were in with me, and so was my husband, Alfie whilst the doctor was talking to me about what happened.

The family thought they were taking me home, but the doctor insisted that I saw a psychiatrist; the whole family was in dilemma. I started feeling very cold and my body was hurting all over and a nurse covered me with an extra blanket. I was lying in the bed shaking and one memory is Alfie standing looking at me. He was crying and asked, "Why? Look what you are doing to us," but I couldn't see how much I was hurting my family. All I could think about was Naylor and my only way out was to be with him.

By now, Alfie's sister, Pauline, had come in to see me. In a kind way, she was telling me off for what I had done and she blurted out, "Do you know that the doctors are going to try to have you sectioned?" Then she gave me a kiss on the face and cuddled me. There was a lot of family outside of the hospital, waiting to do what they could to help. It seemed hours waiting for the psychiatrist and I know one of the family suggested to a nurse that if she could get the on-duty doctor to check me out, they would be able to look after me.

The nurse told them I was not going anywhere. That's when Alfie told me that I was not to tell them I tried to kill myself. He told me, "They will put you in a clinic and I won't be able to get you out." By now, I have been told it was almost certain that I would be sectioned. My daughter, Phyllis, told me to say I hadn't meant to do it. The family were telling me what to say. I was taken to a room to speak to a psychiatrist and Alfie came along with me.

As the psychiatrist started to talk and was asking me about what happened, I could feel Alfie nudge my leg and he mumbled, "Kekker rokka too much, you'll be atched away." This means don't say too much or you will be put away. Alfie took over the conversation and explained to the doctor that we were Romanies and he could not have me put in a clinic at a time like this, and that in our culture it was up to him and the family to take care of me.

The doctor asked Alfie to leave the room so he could speak to me alone. I was asked by the doctor if I meant to take my own life and I remember in my head I wanted to scream out, "Yes, I want to die. I want to be with my baby", and at that point I wouldn't have cared what happened to me, but there was this piece of me deep inside that knew how bad my family was already hurt over losing Naylor, and here was I adding more pain and sorrow on their lives.

The fright on my brother, Dean's face when he found me at my son's graveside with my wrist cut; he had already had heart problems. I could have killed him with shock. All this was going round in my head.

The doctor asked me again, "Did you mean to take your own life?" I told him, "No, it was a cry for help." It was what the family had told me to say, but in no way was I being dominated; it was the Romany way to take care of their own.

The doctor asked me other questions and then he called Alfie back in the room. The doctor agreed with Alfie. He told us that at the place he would have to send me, there were people with lots of different illnesses; some with addictions of drugs and alcohol and many more problems and he knew I was grieving for my son and he felt at this time I should be with my Family.

Before he left, the doctor told me that people who try to take their lives, or who do this as a cry for help, normally succeed by the third time. I don't think I fooled anybody that day. I was signed out in Alfie's care and I had to have follow-up appointments at a clinic. I was also given more tablets to take home with me. I was taken home and I was feeling unwell. Every part of my body was hurting and I couldn't understand why.

I was back to the settee where I had been sleeping since I had lost Naylor. My mum was not told until the family had brought me home, then one of my brothers picked her up and brought her round my house to see me. I heard her voice as she came from the kitchen.

I was propped up on the pillows with a blanket covered over me and as my mum walked into the front room, I put my hand that was bandaged under the blanket so that she couldn't see what I had done. My poor old mum stood in front of me, tears in her eyes. She sat down beside me and said, "My baby, what have you done?" She tried to pull back the blanket gently to look at my hand but I held the blanket tight with my other hand so she could not see It.

I didn't want her to see what I had done. As a mother, grieving for my own child, I knew how much I had hurt her. Here she was, not only knowing how badly I was suffering for the loss of my son, but knowing I was lying there and had tried to take my own life by cutting my wrist. She looked like she was going to crumble with the weight of the world on her shoulders. She looked so helpless and frail. She had always been a strong, upright woman who you could always depend on to pull everything together when things went wrong and a part of me was ashamed for the pain I had caused my mum.

I needed the strength of my mother more
than any time of my life.

CHAPTER TEN

THE DREAM AND HIS PRESENCE

I wasn't allowed to be left alone at all. Alfie made sure of that. Since I'd lost my Naylor my body had felt numb, but after cutting my wrist I seemed to feel every ache and pain and it wasn't my wrist that was hurting that bad, it was my head and all over my body. My daughter gave me my tablets and some painkillers, but I had hardly slept. If I dozed off for an hour, I would wake in horror, the nightmares were so real.

Next morning, Alfie got me an appointment at my own doctor and once we were there, I explained that I was hurting all over. The doctor explained what I had been suffering from. He thought it was post-traumatic shock. He had told Alfie when he first saw me after Naylor's accident that I seemed to be living in my own world. That's when he offered to make arrangements for me to see a psychiatrist, but the family refused at the time. He said that although it was the wrong thing to do, cutting my wrist probably broke the shock.

My body was in a mental breakdown and I was so weak I couldn't even visit my son's grave. I had gone there every day since the funeral; we would always go to our son's grave to light a candle in the evenings and then go back the next morning to put it out. There was this memory in my mind that I always had from the past; a lit candle could keep a spirit with you. Although I was unable to visit my son's grave because I felt so ill, I would tell my husband to make sure we had one burning at home in the evenings and the family would also make sure that they would light one on my son's grave every evening for me. I would lie on the settee, not knowing what day it was most of the time. It was like I was still waiting for my husband, Alfie, to put things right.

During the darkest days.

My daughter has told me that my grandchildren, a couple of them being babies would lie next to me on the settee, drinking their bottles and snuggling up to me, not knowing what was happening. I learned that my grandchildren were so intelligent and sensitive. They could not be sheltered from all that was going on, because a couple of them lived in my house with me and the others were in and out every day, but whenever they were given food, they must have realised that I still wasn't eating properly. They would make sure they fed me with some of theirs, and not once did they ask why my wrist was bandaged. They could have thought of me as this crazy woman after witnessing all the screaming and panic attacks, but they didn't; to them, I was still the Nan they loved so much. A few shadows of my memories are still there, so clear. I was there in body, but in mind, let's just say I wasn't. Did that make me crazy? I suppose it did, with grief.

It wasn't that I loved my son, Naylor, any more than any other one of my children, but we always had this strong 'mother and son' bond. As I said earlier in the book, he always needed that bit more reassurance, and even as a young man, if he had taken the wrong path in life at · some time I was the one he trusted enough to talk to and to help him solve whatever it might have been.

In my mind, I only wanted to be with him. I couldn't stand the thought of him being on his own. I wanted to keep the promise that I'd made him, from a little boy, that I would take care of him when he needed me, but my grandchildren were unaware of this.

My grandson, Naylor, still wanted his sleep over with his Nan and so he did. Although I was so ill and weak and couldn't take care of myself, there must have been a sense of knowing when the children were with me because Naylor slept on the settee with me one night and I did wake up during the night sweating and in a panic, to find my little grandson's arm around my neck.

My daughter, her baby and my sister were all lying on a bed they had made up on the floor next to me. They have told me they were not in a firm sleep; they were just dozing off when they heard me moving about. They both got up from their bed and I told them that my son, Naylor, had been standing in the archway looking down over me and my grandson, Naylor, like he'd come back to see us. I saw him so clearly, but they told me I must have been dreaming.

Then my daughter's baby woke up and straight away he was looking towards the archway and was giggling to himself, putting his hands over his eyes like he was playing peek a boo with someone, but there was no one there. He was doing this for a few minutes and it was like someone had his full attention. Sonny was only two years old and we talk about it still today. My son, Naylor, loved Sonny very much.

Did Sonny see his Uncle Naylor that night? Did he come back to play with him one last time? We will never know for sure. That was the first time of waking up out of my sleep that I was not in a bad nightmare. In my mind, I want to believe that my son came back to see us, but if it was a dream it was a wonderful dream just to feel

My Naylor and his nephew, Sonny. Our family has always lived for it's children.

his presence and see his beautiful face. My daughter and sister settled me back down on the settee and I laid my head on the pillow.

My little grandson, Naylor, snuggled up close and I remember stroking his head gently, knowing how I was feeling this missing of my beautiful and loving son, and the hurt that made my body ache with pain, and here lying beside me was this little boy who had lost his dad at the time of his life just

My Grandson, Naylor and baby granddaughter Christyanna. They helped me more than they will ever know.

as they were doing so many things that father and sons do together, and knowing that the last memory he had of his dad was him going out that morning leaving the house as normal. He had been waiting along with his little brother Razzo for his dad to return home that afternoon, to fill up their swimming pool and their mum was planting flowers in the garden. His world must have been tom apart, as well as mine. I cuddled him close knowing that he was hurting and missing his dad, just as I was my son.

CHAPTER ELEVEN

FEAR

Knowing deep inside, and having pangs of guilt every now and then about how much my husband, my eldest son, my daughter and my grandchildren all needed me, I also saw them break down and cry over losing Naylor, but I still couldn't see beyond the loss of my son in my head. All I could think of was how badly he was hurt that day, and that he would have needed me the most.

Since cutting my wrist, I had not been taken out of the house, not even to visit my son's grave; my body was like it was in meltdown. Every time I thought of anything outside of my home, I would have a panic attack and start shaking. If Alfie had to go out at any time, it would be up to my daughter, Phyllis, and my sister-in-law, whichever one was helping her to take care of me for the day, they would try to get me to have a walk outside with them. I would get to the back door and then panic. It seemed that I was frightened of everything.

The day came when I was supposed to go back to get the stitches out and get my wrist checked, but I would not go out. I was lying on the settee one day when my youngest brother, Dean, came in to see me. He told me he had something wrong with his eye and he needed to go to the hospital to get it checked out. Then he asked me to go with him. I couldn't say no, even though I couldn't even think straight that day.

As we got to the back door, I could feel myself shaking, but I grabbed his hand and walked straight out of the door. My legs felt so weak. We had to walk through the back yard to get to his car and as we got halfway, we had to pass the outside tap. As we got closer, I felt like

I had pins and needles in the side of my face, and my head was tingling. It was so bad that I had to put my hand up to the side of my face so I couldn't see the tap.

Naylor used that tap nearly every time he came to our house for one thing or another and it made memories of Naylor flash in my mind. I couldn't understand what was going on, but my brother, Dean, helped me into his car and I was trembling. As my brother was driving, every time a car passed us I would grab hold of his arm and cower down and scream out. As we pulled up, I asked my brother what we were doing here. We were in a walk-in centre, but he told me it would be too long of a wait at the hospital.

My brother, Dean, was holding onto my arm and we walked to the booking-in desk. The nurse asked for the name and I heard him say, "Mrs. Christine Ball." I said, "It's not me; you need to get your eye checked out." He told me he was sorry the he'd had to tell me a lie, but it was the only way he could think of to get me out the house, and I found out that the rest of the family had known it too.

He told the nurse it was to get my stitches out, and we were staying with friends. He had done all the talking and once we got outside and we were in the car, he told me that he was frightened to take me to the hospital just in case they remembered me. Alfie had to go out and it was up to him to look after me.

I had been in such a state with the fear of going outside and the journey in the car, and I think that was the final straw. He had told me he was so worried they would keep me in and I would end up in a clinic, but after my trip to the walk-in centre, although I was still the same on the journey home, it seemed to break the fear of going outside.

One morning, Alfie walked into the front room with a letter and he looked worried. He told me that it was an appointment for me to see a psychiatrist. It was the follow-up appointment from the hospital and it was one of the conditions when I was allowed home the day I had cut my wrist.

When the day came for me to go to the clinic, my daughter, Phyllis, and my youngest sister-in- law, Sarah Jane, got me dressed; even though months had passed, all my sisters-in-law would still come round every day to help my daughter to take care of me.

Alfie and I went alone, and the drive there was the same as when my brother had taken me to the walk-in centre. As a car came toward us, I would hang on him and cower down in the seat. I had lost my nerve and the fear in my body I cannot describe. As we arrived, Alfie was telling me what to say so that I wouldn't get myself sectioned.

He was so worried that things would go beyond him and he wouldn't be allowed to take care of me the way he believed was the right way of keeping me with him and the family, and he knew how bad my nerves were. I don't know why I remember the clip-clop of my shoes as we were walking in. It sounded like when you hear a little girl walking in her mum's high heels. It was because I had lost so much weight, my feet were slipping in and out of them. It was the first time I had put proper shoes on since the funeral. Alfie was holding my hand and we were showed through, but we had to wait for two doors to be unlocked before we were taken to the psychiatrist's office.

The psychiatrist was a young woman in a smart suit and she asked us to take a seat. It seems strange remembering things that are not that important, same as the noise my shoes had made. She asked me lots of different questions, mostly about my thoughts, and I didn't have to think because I had been told what to say before I got there, but every time I told a lie, the truth would go round in my head. When she asked, "Do you have thoughts of taking your own life?" I was thinking, "Yes, I do". At one point, I did think that if I told the truth the nightmares might stop, maybe she could help me, and although I was telling lies myself, I felt comfortable talking to her. Then she asked me what seemed to me at that time to be the most stupid question I could have heard. She sat across this big desk, twisting a pen, and bearing in mind it was only months since I had lost my son, she asked, "Have the tears stopped yet?" I didn't even answer her. I put my head in my hands. All I could think was, "How could anyone with a heart ask such a stupid question?" Alfie butted in. "Of course, she's still crying. We have lost our son. You don't get over something like that as quickly as you might think."

What little trust I had gained with her was gone in a flash. I didn't really speak much more. The psychiatrist told Alfie that I would be put on a system that they referred to as something like 'an open net' , so that if you felt you needed to speak to someone you could go straight to the clinic. You didn't have to make an appointment. Alfie told her that I was being cared for by him and our family and I had round-the-clock care.

On the way home, Alfie knew I was upset about what was said and he told me, "We have a good family, and I will never let you get put in a clinic and locked away." We arrived home and I was so tired and I felt ill and very weak. My daughter had my bed made on the settee so I lay down and my family was all around me. Nothing had changed. I was still missing my Naylor. I had seen two psychiatrists and although my family was intervening with what I said, it was only because they thought I would be sectioned. As for the psychiatrist asking me if the tears had stopped; inside, for me, the tears would never stop. So who was right? Whatever anyone said wasn't helping me.

CHAPTER TWELVE

THE BOX OF GOODIES

The family were all doing their best, still all rallying round trying to help and to say the right things, which must have been so hard. They were coping day and night, and the same situation would occur, time after time; the panic attacks, waking up screaming for Naylor and hanging on to anyone I could, begging them to help me.

My daughter, Phyllis, was in a terrible state herself. She had two little boys to look after and she was also grieving for her brother who she missed and loved so much. My daughter's husband, Billy, was very good to us all and helped the best he could. My daughter-in-law, Rosy, who is married to my eldest son, Alfie, has told me since that he could not cope with losing his brother and he was taking things more inwardly. Although he lived next door to us he couldn't handle it. When he came to our house to see how I was doing, he would find me lying on the settee, sometimes not even acknowledging that he was there. How sad this must have been for my eldest son. Not only had he lost his brother, but how could he have imagined seeing his mum living in this world with no meaning? It must have seemed to him that I was lost, too.

Naylor's wife, Sue, brought my two young grandsons to see me every day, doing the best she could to help while she was also grieving for the young husband she had lost. We talked about my grandson Razzo's fifth birthday and we were trying to keep things as normal as possible because he was so young. It just didn't seem right without his dad, but we all made a fuss of him. I sat on the chair and thought how sad his little life had been without his dad by his side. He had started school without him, and now his birthday; my heart was aching for him. I was devastated for my beautiful son who had lost his life so young and that he'd miss all the wonderful and important things that were to come in his two young boys' lives in the years to come.

Although I had only been out of the house a few times over the last few weeks, and I was still an emotional wreck when I had to get in a car, I told Alfie that I needed to visit our son's grave, and he agreed to take me.

The evenings were dark. I can remember going past some local houses and there were Christmas lights flashing round a house; no one had mentioned Christmas. Then reality hit. Oh, my God! The thought of Christmas without Naylor! I looked at Alfie as he was driving and asked, "What are we going to do? How will we cope?"

Normally, I would have associated my grandson's birthday with Christmas. My son, Naylor, would always have a laugh with me, and say, "I've got double bubble this month". What he meant was Razzo's birthday and Christmas both in the same month, but I hadn't realised, I was so overtaken by grief. I was in such a panic and I was wondering how his children would feel without him. Alfie carried on driving, his face drained white. I don't think he'd even thought about

Christmas. It seemed that every road we turned down, Christmas was hitting us in the face.

As I walked down to my son's grave, my legs didn't feel like they belonged to me. I felt that I couldn't breathe and I could feel the thud of my heart pounding in my chest. Standing in the dark with just candlelight, my body was overwhelmed with pain. This was to be my path in life from now on.

Because I was still having severe attacks of panic and fear about the accident, I told my daughter I wanted to take flowers to the place where the accident had taken place. I thought it would help to put my mind at rest. I thought, 'That's where my son's last moments of life was'. My husband, Alfie, didn't think it was a good idea, not just before Christmas, but it was decided that a few of the family would go.

We had gone to a garden centre to buy some flowers and as we were walking round I had heard some chimes, and the sound seemed to mean something to me so we bought them. Since I had lost my son, I was drawn to anything that had angels on, whether it was on paper or figurines, and words on cards that people gave me meant so much. So I bought chimes and an angel to take with me and we set off on our journey. It was a long drive and I remember not talking much on the way. I was thinking back on memories from the past.

I was still very uneasy being in a car, and I would cling on to Alfie's arm or slide down in the seat when cars came close. I couldn't tell you where the accident had taken place, and although Alfie had been there before he had taken the wrong road and we got lost. He said, "I think I am miles away," but I knew we were close. I told him I felt numb and said I had this horrible feeling inside. He still thought we were lost and I told him, "I know we are here." As he turned down a long road, he told me, "So we are." We'd come into the road from the opposite direction. I think it was my motherly instinct; I knew my son was hurt there. The road was right outside a farm and as we got out of our car, I couldn't stop crying. Standing so close to where my beautiful boy had lost his life was too much to take in, but it was something I needed to do. It seemed so lonely where the accident had

67

happened. It was in the country and I remember someone from the farm came out to speak to us. He spoke about what happened and he told us he'd done all he could to help on the day of the crash. I asked him if he would tell me where Naylor was lying when they were trying to help him. He walked me to the road and showed me. I was holding the angel that I'd brought so I walked across to the verge from where my Naylor had lain, and I placed it on the grass and laid the flowers. We had also taken a holly wreath and a lantern because I felt I needed to burn a candle there. It meant so much to me at that time.

My husband, Alfie, hung the chimes I had bought as high as he could on a lamp post that was right near where I had placed the angel. Alfie walked across to the other side of the road and he picked something up from Naylor's car. He was upset and crying and so was my daughter, Phyllis. It had upset us all.

I am sure the man we spoke to was called Tony, for some reason that name sticks in my mind, and I asked if he knew if Naylor had spoken any last words. He told me it was all too late. He told me that the young girl who was trying to help Naylor had done everything she could, and said Naylor didn't speak. It was late afternoon, so as we left, we lit the candle and as we drove away I felt part of me was left behind. It was a feeling of wanting to be there, where Naylor had been.

On the way home, we hardly spoke. The shock of being there where Naylor had lost his life was too much for all of us. I had this overwhelming yearning to hold Naylor in my arms and tell him it was all right, that his mum was there with him. I cried all the way home thinking how much he must have needed me that day.

I had thoughts of Naylor asking for me even though I had been told that he didn't speak. On the journey home, I closed my eyes for a while and I could see the angel and hear the soft rings of the chimes and the flickering light of the candle, and even though I was in disbelief of God, and I felt like a traitor asking for help, I prayed and prayed for him to take care of my baby. That journey was to become one of many. On every occasion, I had to go back to that sad place and lay flowers and light a candle.

Everything I did at that time involved Naylor, like visiting his grave or lighting candles, and became a ritual. My house became a shrine to my son. I had photos everywhere as soon and as I found a new photo, I would get one of the family to have it enlarged and get it framed. About the same time, I started wearing Naylor's T-shirt that he had been wearing the day of the accident. I also had his trainers and socks and would not let anyone touch them. Because Naylor was always around my house most days, he would bathe and shave at our house sometimes. Every now and then, I would go in this frantic mode of trying to find anything he had used or touched. I collected the shaving brush, shaving cream, hairbrush, anything. I even had a jar of his favourite Branston pickle in the fridge and no one was allowed to touch it. It must have looked to others that I had gone crazy, and maybe I had.

In all the years that had passed, for weeks before Christmas, I would take time over buying and choosing the right presents for all my children, and I made sure that our Christmas tree was put up early so everyone got into the spirit. Every year, I had a box under the stairs and in the few weeks leading up to Christmas I put different things in it, like sweets and a few cans of beer. I would fill it with loads of different stuff. This box was for Naylor, because as I said earlier in the book, he needed more reassurance from me sometimes and I think this was my way to show him that I knew that, and how much I cared for him. My other two children knew about this box, but never made a fuss; they would never say that Naylor had more than Them.

A few days before Christmas, I would tell Naylor there was a box for him under the stairs, and he would collect his box of goodies. He always gave me a kiss and a big hug, and he always said, "Thanks, my old gel."

If the other children were there when he collected his box, he would hold it in his arms and start laughing. He knew what they would say to him. 'There he goes Mum's pet!' It was our joke. All my children knew I loved them all the same; there was never any doubt there. These memories would flash through my mind and now, all I was doing was going to visit my Naylor's grave.

I can remember Alfie saying that we had to sort flowers out for Christmas, but I felt so sad and lonely, all I wanted was to be with Naylor. How could I leave him on his own? Christmas seemed to get closer and the family made sure that our grandchildren got their Christmas trees up, and tried to make things as normal as possible. My husband, Alfie, gave money to our daughter, Phyllis, and our two daughters-in-law to make sure that our grandchildren had got their presents, but in our house, Christmas had been cancelled. It was like it didn't exist.

CHAPTER THIRTEEN

THE FLASH BACK

Christmas was a couple of weeks away. There were Christmas lights in every road we went down. People were celebrating and we were lost in time. I didn't know how I got from here to there, time had gone on and we were all oblivious. In the meantime, my mum had been unwell again and my sister had made her a hospital appointment.

Being the eldest daughter in a Romany family, I knew that although I was grieving for my son and I was still unstable, it was my place to go with my mum and sister, Charmain, to the hospital. Our mum was a very private woman and we all knew it. She would only allow her daughters to speak to the doctors about her health. So I had a long lecture from my husband about trying not to worry about anything else that day, and not to do anything silly, and to be there for my mum.

My sister, Charmain picked me up on the day of my mum's appointment and I had taken pills before we left for the hospital, to help me to cope with the journey. On the way to the hospital my mum was talking to me, asking if I felt all right. I was lying back on the seat of my sister's car and let's just say that my brain was on a different level. I couldn't get Naylor off my mind and I felt very nervous as we were driving.

We finally got to the hospital and I can remember looking around the waiting room, and I must have just sat there staring at people. They all looked uneasy and I thought how worried they looked. I began to notice doctors and nurses walking through corridors, just doing their everyday things and straight away, it brought flashes back about Naylor and I started to feel sick and shaky so I told my sister that I had to use the toilets. I just needed to get out. I found the toilets and I went into a cubicle. I was trembling with nerves and I thought I was going to be sick, but as I leaned over the toilet, I fell to my knees. The panic and the fear and fright were back. My body was in a cold sweat. I can only say that the noise in my head was unbearable and my mind seemed out of control.

I had flashes of the day of the accident, and how Alfie and I were running through the corridors of the hospital trying to find out where our son, Naylor, had been taken. My husband, Alfie, had given me a couple of tablets to take with me just in case I needed them. I fumbled to get them out of my pocket and I knew I wasn't supposed to take the two of them, but with the fear I was in, I put them both in my mouth.

I got myself up from the floor and out of the cubicle, and then washed my face in the sink and sorted myself out. That was the first time I had dealt with the fear and panic on my own and I felt stronger in myself, knowing I had got through it. I walked back out to my mum and my sister and they were chatting. They asked if I was all right as I sat down and I never told them about the attack of fear that I'd had.

I can only remember that I sat as close to my mum as I could get, and leaned my head on her shoulder. I needed my mum so much. My head was hurting and I felt dizzy.

My mum was called in, so my sister and I both got up from our seats and walked in with her to see the doctor. As I said earlier, my mum was very old-fashioned, but she was very polite and well-mannered when talking to doctors and nurses. I can remember her words to us children when we were growing up: "Please and thank you don't cost you anything."

As the doctor was talking, my mum blurted out, "Sorry, doctor. I just want to let you know if you've got anything you want to tell me, I don't want to know today."

You could say she was old-school. She sounded like a little girl being told something she didn't want to hear. Then she said, "but you can talk to my daughters." She said "thank you" to the doctor, and said she would be waiting outside the office. The doctor told my sister and I to make another appointment and we were to leave our mum at home on the next visit because it would be Christmas week. We walked out of the hospital and our mum seemed like she didn't want to talk about it so we left it. She seemed more concerned about me and if I was all right. I remember feeling so sick knowing that my mum was ill again.

During the following week, my mum came to see me as normal and it was so close to Christmas. We were organising flowers for Naylor and it didn't feel right. I remember Alfie asking what colour flowers I wanted and in an instant, I said, 'red'. I knew that red is the colour associated with Christmas, but it was nothing to do with that. When my Naylor was little he had red wellies that he loved, and for some reason my mind was wandering in memories of back then. I wasn't really thinking of the flowers.

The week passed, and my sister, Charmain, and I went alone as the doctor had asked. I knew my mum was ill, but since I had lost Naylor my brain seemed to be switched off from anything other than him. As we walked in the doctor's office, Charmain asked the doctor how our mum was doing. He had told us the scan did not look good, and that the cancer was back. Thinking back now, I was there in body but my mind was like a sponge. It would absorb things, and that's where it would stay, hidden away. I know I wasn't in sound mind, because how could I have been when a doctor tells you, "If this were my mum, I would make this Christmas the best, and one to remember." I looked at my sister, who was crying, but I felt stunned and I didn't speak much.

I remember my sister Charmain explaining to the doctor that I had lost my son and that I couldn't cope with what I was going through, let alone more bad news. He told me he was sorry to hear that, and he told us he was also sorry that he didn't have any better news, and to try to enjoy Christmas with our mum.

We travelled home devastated, not speaking much. Once home, we told our two brothers, Lenny and Dean and my sister explained the news as best she could to the family. Our mum asked what the doctor had said and we told her that things were going all right and that the doctor wanted to see her in the New Year.

Although my mum was ill, she was a very strong woman, walking about and still trying to be there for her family, and she would come to my house every day to be with me and help the best she could. I know in my own heart that my mum knew more about what was going on than she had let on to us, but thinking back, I don't think I could take in the news that it would be the last Christmas I'd have with my mum.

CHAPTER FOURTEEN

THE SADDEST CHRISTMAS

It was a couple of days before Christmas Eve and the day we had decided to go to the cemetery to take Naylor's flowers to lay them on his grave. I was feeling so down and so nervous. Alfie and I had a cross in holly with fresh red roses in and we had vases of roses that covered his grave. All the family had brought their flowers and it was heartbreaking seeing the flowers, there were so many.

My son, Alfie, and my daughter, Phyllis, and my son, Naylor's two little boys, all had their own special floral tributes that meant something to them. His wife was the only one to lay pink roses; it was her way of showing her love for him. We had been going to and from the cemetery twice a day.

I couldn't sleep at night and the only way I can describe how my memories flowed is that my head was like a merry-go-round; It span around and around and then another memory would jump on board, and then it would spin out of control. My memories would be from when Naylor was a newborn, right through his childhood to becoming a young man, and then the day of the accident would send me into a frenzy.

Christmas day arrived. Normally, we would wake up to the smell of turkey cooking and the excitement of Christmas would fill the air. There would be presents under the tree standing tall and sparkling with a magical glow. By mid-morning our Christmas dinner would be cooking and I'd be ready to be host to my family on that special day, but not this year, or in years to come.

I had slept hardly at all on Christmas Eve. I would doze in and out of sleep and most of the time I'd think I was dreaming, and then the fear would hit me, knowing that I really had lost my Naylor. By morning, I was a wreck. I had taken so many tablets to help me through this terrible time that on Christmas morning I felt a bit out of it, but it didn't take my pain away. I can remember sitting up and looking over at my husband, Alfie, who sat with his head in his hands. As he lifted his head and looked over at me, his face was filled with despair and pain. We were both sobbing our eyes out and I remember Alfie helping me, more than himself. I think we had a cup of tea and then went straight to visit Naylor's grave.

As we were driving, my mind was on his two little boys. I couldn't imagine how they were feeling, waking up to open their presents and their dad not being there. Those poor little boys, and their mum trying to hold things together. How sad life had become. As we got to the cemetery, I was in a panic. I could hear the tinkling of the chimes that we had hung from a tree at the graveside, but where was his box of goodies? Where were his presents? I missed him so much.

My baby; I needed to hold him and hug him tight. Before I knew it, I was in bits at his grave as I looked at the flowers that covered the area surrounding it. As I stood staring, I was thinking, 'All these flowers. What does it all mean?' In my heart, I knew that if I had laid one rose on my beautiful son's grave it would have meant as much as a thousand blooms. My husband and I left to go home. It was still very early and by the time we arrived home, we were distraught. A little while later, our other children came round to see us and once our grandchildren had opened their presents, we all went back to the cemetery to take small tokens of love for Naylor. It was so sad to see all the family standing around, and his two boys, who should have been sharing a wonderful day with their dad, looked so sad. By this time, a lot more family members had arrived to support us and be there for Naylor.

My eldest son and daughter-in-law, who lived right next door to us, had cooked Christmas dinner for all our grandchildren and close family. Alfie and I sat in our house alone. Our son and daughter brought our dinner round to us and placed the dinners on our laps as we sat in our front room. When they came back, we were still sitting and had not eaten anything, and we both apologised for not eating the dinner, but he had known how we were feeling. After dinner, just as the evening was falling, we all went back to the cemetery and lit more candles.

I felt so hurt leaving my Naylor on his own as I walked halfway down the path towards the gate to leave and I had this feeling of him watching me walk away, but as I turned all I could see was the flickering of the candles.

That night, our son, Alfie, and our daughter, Phyllis, and their families came round and sat with us. I can remember my son, Alfie, making me a drink. He told me, "I know you will like this." It was a Bailey's Cream and brandy and it was my eldest son's favourite Christmas drink. I don't know why that sticks in my mind.

The following days passed and then it was New Year's Eve, what should have been a happy occasion. We went to the cemetery throughout the day and I told the family that I wanted to be with Naylor at midnight.

I wanted to be with him. I didn't want him to be alone. The family agreed, and we went to the cemetery about 11.30 that night so we could see the New Year in with Naylor.

When we got there, we found that other people had already been. Some of his mates had taken drinks, had drunk a few mouthfuls of their drink, and then stood the bottles on Naylor's grave. One stood out to me among the rest. It was a glass with a gold rim around it, that was half-filled with champagne. Someone had taken the time to walk down to the cemetery that night with that glass. I felt overwhelmed with pride that his mates thought of him on that special night, and had all taken the time to visit their old friend.

I was so moved on finding the glass with the champagne in it that I asked around to find out who had left it there. Who it was soon came to light. It had been one of his oldest friends from childhood and I know he won't mind me saying his name - it was Golias Beldom. I left the glass there over Christmas and then I brought it home with me and placed it in my cabinet with things that Naylor had brought me over the years. It still sits there among the things that I will treasure forever. Golias was also one of Naylor's friends who helped to carry him to his place of rest on the day of the funeral.

We stood at the graveside and we each had a drink in our hand. As midnight came, there were fireworks exploding in the air and we all took a sip from our drinks and then placed them on Naylor's grave. We stood in silence and I remember being in disbelief of what I was Doing.

'My poor baby' , that's all I could think and I could have sat there all night with him. We could hear laughter coming from the houses across the street as people were celebrating the New Year in with their families, and I dreaded walking away and leaving him.

My thoughts were disturbing. Although I was standing next to my family that loved me so much and were doing everything they could to help me, I still felt my place as a mother was to be with Naylor, and in my mind, he was the one who was lonely and on his own. I seemed to drift off into my own world. I had flashes of Naylor that day. I cradled his head in my arms knowing he was hurt so bad. In my head, I was telling him that I was going to be with him to take care of him and love him. That as his mum, he knew he could trust me as he always did, so on that night standing at his graveside, I had it firmly in my head that I would be with him soon.

CHAPTER FIFTEEN

THE INQUEST

A new year had begun but nothing had changed. My life still felt in turmoil. How do you go on living in a world that doesn't seem real, and everything good is missing? My life felt like a jigsaw with a piece missing, and it was never going to be complete again. The missing piece was lost for ever and, in my mind, so was my life.

Time passed. One day led into another and I seemed to be lost. The families were still taking it in turns to come around to our house and help as much as they could, even though they all had their own families to run. One day, my husband, Alfie, came in and sat on the settee, reading a letter. I heard him say, "I can't believe it! How on earth have I let this happen?" I think it might have been my daughter, or my sister, in the room with us who asked what was wrong. He told them that the letter was from our landlords and we were nearly £2000 in arrears with our rent. We all just sat, and then realised that with all the trauma we had been going through, nobody had thought to pay the rent. It was the last thing on our minds. It shows how life was passing by, and we weren't thinking about whatever came with it. Alfie got on the phone and explained what had happened in the family, and it was sorted out, but he had to try to go back to work. He always made sure that there was someone to take care of me. I told my husband that I'd had enough of being baby-sat, but every day someone would be there.

Alfie was still worried because I wasn't eating much, so I had another appointment with my doctor. Once we were at the doctor's, Alfie told him that he was worried about me and said I was barely eating enough to keep myself alive and asked if there was anything he could Prescribe.

The doctor put me on the scales, and then said, "You need to start eating properly, Christine, because you will become so weak, and if you become ill you won't get over it". In my mind, that's what I wanted and I told the doctor that I never felt hungry, so he looked at Alfie and said, "There is something you can try. Buy a bottle of red wine and give Christine a small glass in the evenings with a sandwich." He told us that sometimes, when you drink red wine it can make you feel a bit hungry. It was more friendly advice than professional. He was just trying to help. The doctor told us to come back in a month and he would weigh me. Alfie and I left the surgery with a prescription for antidepressants and some other pills.

After we got home, Alfie went back to the chemist to get my prescription and that evening I'd forgotten what the doctor had said, until Alfie came into the room with a glass of red wine and a sandwich which he placed on a table next to me. I can remember telling Alfie that I didn't like the taste of the wine, but he told me to drink a little and have a small bite of the sandwich, so I did as my husband asked.

Every evening, Alfie would put a small glass of wine with a sandwich in front of me, and after a few days, I seemed to get a taste for the wine. Then I would ask my husband for another glass, and before long I was drinking a bottle of wine every night. I think because I would pick over the sandwich, my husband Alfie felt it was an improvement and didn't see any wrong in me drinking a bottle of wine and for me it was something to take me further away from this horrible nightmare.

A month passed and it was time to go back for a visit to the doctor. As we walked in, the doctor asked how I was doing and Alfie told him that I was still having really bad attacks of fear and that they seemed to come during the day, and the night. He was worried that it wasn't getting any better. The doctor once again said, "Maybe it would be a good idea to talk to a psychiatrist."

Alfie told the doctor that I was being taken care of by the family and him, but the doctor told us to think about it. He asked me to get on the scales so he could check on my weight and he looked very pleased. "That's brilliant, Christine," he said. "You've put two pounds on." I looked over at Alfie, who looked very pleased with himself because he had been the one coaching me to eat the sandwich and drink the wine."Oh, by the way," said the doctor. "How are you getting on with your glass of wine? Did you try it? It looks like you've been doing something right." With that, Alfie struck up and said very proud of himself, "Oh, she is doing very well, doctor. She's drinking a bottle of wine every night now, and eating most of her sandwich." The doctor stood up from his chair, looking very concerned, and said in a disturbed voice, "Christine! No, that's too much! I told you one small glass with a sandwich in an evening. You can't drink that amount. It's bad for you; think of the tablets you are taking!" Alfie promised the doctor that I would cut down to one glass a night, or maybe every other night.

As the days and weeks passed, I missed my son more than ever and couldn't see any future without him. I longed to see his beautiful, shy smile; I missed that cuddle when he walked into my kitchen and wanted a sandwich. I was out of my mind with grief. My husband, Alfie, was trying the best he could to carry on with work and to help look after me, but we couldn't seem to talk about Naylor without arguing. He was dealing with his grief differently to me and I just wanted to talk about Naylor all the time, but he couldn't so my drinking and taking more pills seemed the only way that I could cope.

We were all dreading the day of the inquest into the accident, and Alfie had made it clear that he couldn't go to hear about what had happened that day, but as a mother I needed to know what had happened to my son. I just had to know what had gone wrong that day. That caused a conflict between us because my husband was worried and he told me that I was too much of an emotional wreck to sit and listen to the details.

My daughter, Phyllis, had been dealing with phone calls from the coroner's office and one afternoon she came to me and told me that the date of the hearing had arrived. Alfie stood by his word and said he was sorry, but he couldn't go with me so it was decided that Phyllis and I, and my sister, Charmain, would go.

On the morning we set out, I was trembling just thinking about what was going to be said and it was a long journey, which seemed to make things worse. I had taken tablets before we left but they didn't take away that awful feeling of knowing and remembering what had happened on that dreadful day. I felt sick with nerves, and as we arrived and parked the car I was looking around as we were walking in, knowing that the woman who had been driving the other car would be here somewhere. I was in a turmoil of mixed feelings inside me, but we walked in.

We had to wait to be called, and I remember thinking how I needed my husband to be with me. As a Romany couple, no matter how bad things got, the way we had been brought up from both our families was that you always pulled the same way, and in our world, the man was always the protector - but not this time. My husband was heartbroken himself, and needed to handle his grief his way, but I needed him more than ever. For the first time, our two worlds collided.

A lady walked over and asked if we were there for the inquest and then took us into what looked like a courtroom. We sat in the front seats, and there was a woman sitting at a desk. I heard her say, "This is the inquest of Naylor Ball", and just hearing my son's name put waves of fear in my stomach. I can't remember how it started, but when the coroner was called up to speak and tell of my son's injuries, I sat staring at him. I will never forget his face, it's like it is painted in my mind. As he was asked, he told of my son's fatal injuries; he went through every one in great detail, even an appendix scar, and right down to a graze on his knee. As he described each injury, I could visualise them in my mind and I felt like I was going to faint. All I could think of was how badly my poor baby was hurt.

Although this is a true story, I can't go into any more detail because I have the greatest respect for my husband and it would be betraying his wishes of not wanting to know everything that was said at the inquest - and he might well read this book one day. The other driver was called to the stand and I sat with my head bowed down, I could not bring myself to look directly at her, but from the comer of my eye I saw a small frail figure of a woman. My sister later told me that she had looked traumatised. She and her 14-year-old son had been driving along what would have been a main road, and I remember her saying that the sun had been very bright that day, but it hadn't affected her vision of the road. She had to be given water because she started to choke as she was talking, and then she said that Naylor's car had come out straight across from a side road, and she'd had no chance to stop. Then a technical police officer spoke and showed photos of both cars, but I couldn't look. He said that if he had been driving Naylor's car, he also would have gone straight across the road because there had been no major halt signs at the top of it. The officer told us the speed at which both cars had been travelling; the woman's car at about 45mph and Naylor's at 33mph. He said that if Naylor had been going a bit faster he would have probably got across the road. He hadn't known he'd been approaching a major road ahead until it was too late and both cars collided.

The woman and her son, and Naylor's friend, Fred, were all taken to hospital with injuries. Naylor had been the only one to have lost his life. The verdict was 'accidental death due to multiple injuries'. I think we were the last ones to leave the court. I felt so helpless, but every time my son's name was spoken, no matter how painful it was to hear, in my heart, as his mother who had brought him into this world, I had felt it was my place to be there on the closure of his life.

My young daughter and my sister were so distraught that the journey home was almost silent. By this time I felt very ill and my sister had given me a couple of my tablets. I was still very nervous of being in a car, but after sitting and listening to what had happened to my son deep fear took over my body. I tried to close my eyes, but every time I did I could imagine the injuries that we were told my son had, and that he was only seconds from getting across that road.

It's so hard when you're dying inside to try to live on. My disbelief in God was now greater, and my question was, 'Why, God? Why my son? Please, tell me why'. I felt I had nothing left without my belief and my mind was like a merry-go-round - it was like my head was spinning. One minute my head would flash with the most recent memories of what I had just heard the coroner say, and the next, I wandered back to my son's childhood. It seemed that every time I had this spiral of memories, I would go back through the steps of Naylor's life. We had to travel on a motorway to get home and it triggered a memory of when my children were all young. Naylor loved the Army and if he spotted the Army lorries on manoeuvre he would shriek with delight and he'd say, "Catch them up, Dad! Come on, Dad - faster." My husband would try to get as close has he could and my children loved to wave at the soldiers, especially Naylor.

As a little boy, Naylor couldn't pronounce anything that began with the letter A and when he saw the Army he meant to say to his brother, "Look Alf! There's the Army", but his words came out as, "Look Falf! There's the Farmy." He called his elder brother, 'Falf' throughout

Naylor and his big brother 'Falf'.

their younger years. Looking back on those days, I can still hear that excitement in his voice and the wonderful, innocent look that can only come from such beauty within a child. He was my beautiful, fun-loving little boy who grew into a wonderful young man, but sometimes even the most wonderful memories of my children all being together and so happy became too much to bear and my mind hit back to reality and the unbearable world that I had to live in.

It was late by the time we arrived home that afternoon, and all I wanted to do was visit my son's grave. My husband asked if I was all right, but the inquest wasn't spoken about. It was very hard, but that's how it had to be.

My son, Naylor, as the happy little boy I'll always hold in my heart.

My three, posing together.

CHAPTER SIXTEEN

TWO HEARTS BEAT AS ONE

My health seemed to spiral downhill. No matter which tablets I was prescribed by doctors, none could take away the panic and the fear I was living with every day. I had still carried on drinking wine in the evenings, but it had never taken away my pain. It just seemed to cushion my mind from the heavy blows of anguish for a short time, and then it would hit me with vengeance. My emotions were all over the place and I was still so agitated that nothing helped. I couldn't cope with everyday life, and things had become like rituals. Although I had told my husband that I didn't need to be baby-sat, he still insisted and on the days when he had to work he would make sure that either our daughter, Phyllis, was with me, or one of our family members.

On this particular day, it was my sister, Charmain, who was sitting with me, and she was concerned. Since I'd had lost Naylor, I didn't care about how I looked or how I dressed, so long as my clothes were black, because as Romanies, if a family member dies we wear black clothing for a year to show our respect. Her concern was about my hair; it is very dark and before I lost my son I probably would have had the front section of my roots dyed every six weeks or so, but for some reason the roots were no longer grey, they had gone white and not only in the front section, but right through my head. You can imagine what I looked like, with black hair and white roots, and all my family had mentioned it, so my sister was determined to get me to the hairdressers to get my hair sorted. Although I didn't feel like going I said I'd go with her, but on one condition.

Since the day I had cut my own wrist, Alfie would only allow me to hold a couple of tablets at a time, and whoever was sitting with me took charge of the rest. One of the tablets I was taking at that time, the doctors had called 'blueys' they were little blue tablets and very strong. My one condition was that my sister brought my blueys with her, just in case I had a panic attack, and she agreed to do so, so we went along to the hairdressers I'd been using before I lost my son. I knew all the girls there and they were always very friendly towards me, and had sent flowers when they'd heard about Naylor. Before I walked in I told my sister to make sure that no one spoke to me because I couldn't handle ordinary conversation. I just wanted to have my hair done and then leave, and that's just what I did, although normally it would not have been in my nature to do this.

I didn't feel right as we were leaving. I was shaking and I think it had been too much for me. All the time I was there, I was thinking of Naylor. There was a restaurant next door with chairs and tables outside, and I had to sit down and rest on them. I seemed to have lost my nerve, and the fear of doing things that I would have done normally was all too much. My head was in a frenzy, and the panic of losing my son was back. My sister told me later that I was telling her I was going to smash my head through a big glass window because I couldn't stand what was going around in it. I told her I needed my tablets to stop my head spinning and she gave me two. I also demanded an alcoholic drink. I told her I just wanted the pain to stop. I was begging her to help me.

My sister was reluctant to get me a drink because she knew I had been left in her care and she was worried, but I was in such a state and causing such a scene that she bought me one. I can remember being in the car on the way home and, out of the blue, for some reason I told my sister I needed to get a tattoo of Naylor's name. I had this urge and I needed to do something.

I can remember crying, begging her to help me and I saw her use her phone but I didn't know who she'd rung, but she finally agreed.

We arrived at the tattoo shop and as we walked in I must have looked in a bad state because one man came out to see us, looked at me standing there crying and went back out through a door. He must have thought I was crazy. Then another man came out and my sister told him about what had happened to Naylor. We sat down and discussed it and he told me it might be too much for me to get a tattoo because I wasn't very well. I told him I would be all right. By now, more of my family had walked through the door - my two sisters-in-law - and they both tried talking to me, trying to stop me, but it was no good I had made up my mind, and I now knew who my sister had rung. I had taken my jacket off and my arms were so thin and frail, but we sat down with the man who designed and did my tattoo. I now know him as Lloyd and he has become a good friend of the family over the years.

I didn't flinch as the tattoo was being done, but my sister said there was a lot of bleeding and she sat there in tears, but my tattoo meant so much to me; it seemed that all I had was words. I chose 'NAYLOR. LOVE YOU ALWAYS. TWO HEARTS BEAT AS ONE'. In my heart, that's how I felt. All the time my heart was beating, so was his, and I would never let him go. We left the tattoo shop and went home. The family was in shock, and stunned by what I had done, but they have all grown to love it.

When my poor sister left my house, she went back to our mum's place, fell in her arms, and broke down and said how sad it had left her, to have to see me become so distraught doing an ordinary task like getting my hair done, and then begging and crying to have a tattoo of my son's name on my arm. Without knowing, and through no fault of my own, I was hurting my family, especially my mum who had by now become very ill.

Alfie.

CHAPTER SEVENTEEN

POISONED BY GRIEF

My mum was back and forth to the hospital, but trying to stay strong. She still came to sit with me, and there would always be flowers on my windowsill, or a pot plant that she had brought. She loved to see my grandchildren when she was around my house, and always made a fuss of them.

Naylor's two little boys came to stay every weekend and even though it was not like it used to be, they loved to stay. I would do my best to make things as normal as I could, but watching those two boys without their dad was tearing me apart. I would sit and try to think how many mothers before me had gone through what I was feeling, and wonder how they coped. I couldn't live from day to day and was struggling to get through one hour at a time without getting hit by waves of panic because of my son's death.

Words can never describe the hurt and pain that comes from deep within your soul; grief runs through your veins like poison, with no cure in sight. Imagine you are at the seaside, nice and calm, just out in the sea where you feel comfortable. Suddenly, out of nowhere, this giant wave hits you so hard that it knocks you straight off balance and you go under, deeper and deeper, until you're swamped with water, up your nose, in your mouth. You're in shock. You hear loud noises in your ears, and see flashes in your head, and you can't see properly, and you're struggling, but you can't swim, and you can't breathe and you're so weak that you can't help yourself. You're drowning.

Alfie. Taking care of Naylor's two little boys.

This is how I feel every time I get those unbearable attacks of panic and fear, but I am drowning in pain and being poisoned by grief. If I was at the seaside before I lost Naylor, and someone had asked me to read the words that I have just written, it would have put a fear in me and I would not have wanted to go near the sea. That's how I felt about life every time I had an attack, or even thought of what had happened to my son. I didn't want to be here. Living in this world seemed impossible.

The day before Naylor's birthday, the first one we had to face without him, I was sitting on the bench next to Naylor's grave whilst my husband was getting water from the tap. He looked so lonely and hurt and I could see the pain in his face, and as he walked back to the bench I could see he had been crying. My first instinct was to comfort him and tell him we would be all right, but I couldn't because it wasn't going to be all right. How do you come back from this? How do you say it and not mean it? In my head, I was still waiting for him, as the man of our family, to sort out this trauma we were living in.

I begged him to help me, and he would try to talk to me and say we had to be strong for our other children. He said we will never forget Naylor and he will always be with us. He even told me he felt Naylor's spirit with him all the time, but I couldn't seem to talk to him. It would always end up with me screaming and crying, telling him I couldn't live like this, and that I didn't want to be here. I wanted to die. I would say, "How many times do I have to tell you. My Naylor needs me." My husband would always walk away from me, distraught.

This same argument would occur every time. Alfie was dealing with his grief in his way, as a father, and I was trying to deal with mine as a mother, and my world was tumbling down around me. The hardest thing was, we both loved our son unconditionally, but grief was pulling us apart without us even realising it was

My Darling Alfie and Beautiful Son Naylor. So happy in the sun.

happening. I seemed to have been living in a bubble and I was pushing away those who loved me. It seemed that every time we got through one big traumatic occasion, there was another one waiting. This time, as I said, it was Naylor's birthday, and it was upsetting for all the family.

I planned to plant a tree in my son's memory, at the place where he had lost his life. It had now become one of my rituals that I needed to visit this spot and light a candle there. My sister-in-law, Sarah Jane, took me to the garden centre and helped me to choose a couple

The birthday flowers.

of trees; a magnolia because when it blooms it has beautiful white flowers, and a weeping female, which is an evergreen. I also brought a magnolia tree to plant in my own garden so that when my one at home was in bloom, I knew there would be flowers at home and far away in his memory. My mum heard we were going to plant a tree for Naylor and she walked into my house that evening with a little bag in her hand, and asked if we could do something special for her. In the bag was a small fir tree that she had taken from my dad's grave, and she told us she would like it planted with ours. It was a token from her and my dad, and we told her we would be sure to plant the tree for her.

That evening, Naylor's two young boys came over and we spoke about their dad's birthday. Although they were young, they still understood and were eager to get their dad something. They especially wanted to get birthday cards, so to make it feel more special I asked them if they wanted to make their own. They were over the moon and couldn't wait to start. I was falling apart myself and it probably would have been easier for me to let them buy a card, but I knew how much it would help them to be doing something special for their dad, who they were missing so much.

They chatted to me whilst we were making the card. My son's eldest, was saying, "Me dad will like this, won't he Nan?" and his youngest son, Razzo, told me that his dad was a star in the sky. I said, "Yes, he his, my two beautiful boys, so when you look up in the sky at night, he's the

The boys' cards for their dad.

one that will shine so bright." The boys loved to talk about their dad all the time. I used to tell Razzo that he would always be his dad's baby boy, and say to Naylor, "You will always be your dad's big boy." They would give me a cheeky smile and have a little giggle. I felt I was choking, and it was killing me to fight back the tears, but when I was with Naylor's two little boys, I felt I had to be at my strongest. We talked about their dad's birthday picnic in the park, the last one we had shared together with him and my mind wandered back to that beautiful memory.

To celebrate Naylor's birthday, we had gone out to Black Park for the day. Naylor had been estranged from his wife, Sue, for a short while so my daughter Phyllis and I met Naylor there. Phyllis had taken her two sons, Naylor's two boys were there, my nephew, Sean and niece, Lana. The sun was shining and my Naylor had his T-shirt off, folded and tucked hanging from his back pocket.

As Naylor was walking, he picked up his little boy, Razzo, and put him on his shoulders, holding his legs with one hand, and he had hold of his elder son's hand with the other. Naylor was tall and very dark as he was walking just in front of me he turned back to speak to

Naylor's two beautiful Sons.

me. I always noticed from when he was a little boy that he had a shy look about him and an amazing smile. I thought how handsome he looked and what a wonderful father he was to his boys.

We walked around the park and found a table. We had taken loads of food and made a joke that my son, Naylor, had eaten most of the cakes. He was such a laugh and a joy to be with. Naylor took the children to look at the water; he loved all his nieces and nephews and always had time for them. We all had a lovely lunch and then while the children were playing, my daughter and I chatted with Naylor about his troubles, as families do. As he sat across the table from me, talking to my daughter, they were laughing and joking and then Naylor took all the children and bought them ice creams. We had a wonderful day, and each and every one of us who shared that special day with Naylor will be able to hold those beautiful memories close to our hearts forever.

It was the morning of Naylor's birthday and his two little boys had stayed over at our house the night before so they could be with us that morning. My husband made their breakfasts and I had taken extra tablets to help me keep calm in front of my grandchildren. Naylor's boys had the card they'd made and their flowers ready to visit their

97

dad's grave.

Once there, we all laid our flowers down and lit our candles. Naylor and Razzo were taking their time in finding a place for the card they had made for their dad, and it had been hard helping the boys make it, but just by watching them find a special place for it, I knew it meant so much to them. My heart missed a beat, just knowing that they felt they had done something special for their dad.

The rest of the family arrived, and the children wandered around the cemetery as they always did, in a little group. I had an empty feeling inside, and my husband hardly spoke, he just sat staring at our son's grave. We left the cemetery and told the rest of the family that we would meet them back there later.

There were two things we had to do, and to be honest it was what I wanted to do. First of all, Alfie and I, our daughter, Phyllis, and her two boys, and Naylor's two boys all went back to Black Park in remembrance of Naylor's birthday. We

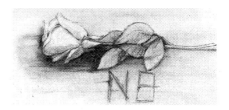

Illustration of the rose.

walked round and sat on the same bench as we had on my Naylor's last birthday. My daughter and Naylor's two boys scratched N-B on the table, and I laid a white rose on there, next to it. Ten years have passed, and I still lay a white rose on the same table every birthday, and the N-B is still there.

We then set out on our way to the place where our son had lost his life, to plant the trees we had bought in his memory. We had a long journey in front of us, but we didn't say much, we were both very distraught and had been holding in our emotions in front of Naylor's little boys whilst they'd stayed over with us for the night. Just watching them together, playing and talking as children do, seemed to make reality hit home even more.

As we got further into the journey, we spoke of how Naylor's boys had tried to find the special place for their card and how important it was to them. I also said I was worried over my eldest son, and my daughter, and I didn't know what to do. Alfie told me that I had to try to pull myself together, to eat a bit more food, and try to look after myself. He said we had to pull together as a family and I must try to be strong.

I'd been holding myself together as much as I could that day, and I told him so, and then I started to cry and said that I missed my baby; I wanted to hold him, and cuddle him, and tell him I loved him on his birthday. I got these strong, overwhelming urges as a mother, to be with my Naylor. Then I could feel the fear and panic set in, and I couldn't stop crying. I ended up in a frenzy.

By now, Alfie had raised his voice, telling me to stop and that I was sending myself mad. He tried to say it how it was, but I didn't want to know. I screamed at my husband, telling him that I was waiting for my Naylor and that I would always be waiting for him. Then Alfie said, "You've got to understand. He can't come home! You are sending yourself crazy."

I begged him, time and time again, to help me. I screamed so loudly, telling him that I couldn't live without my boy, that I didn't want to live like this. I had to take extra tablets to calm my head down. It had got so bad that we couldn't seem to speak a few words about Naylor without it turning into us arguing. The rest of the journey was silent, but every now and then, my husband asked me if I was all right. He looked so worried.

We arrived at the place where the accident took place, and we were very upset at being there. Alfie was getting the trees out of the car, ready to plant, and I was standing next to a little angel that I'd placed there on the visit before. I just stood crying, looking out at the spot where my Naylor had laid on that fateful day, and my body was shaking with fear; everything was going through my head in flashes of memory.

I could see the crash, even though I hadn't been there. In my head, I could hear the coroner telling us of Naylor's injuries on that day, and it all seemed so real. The road was fast; cars were passing by and I saw a lorry coming toward me. I was standing on the verge, a couple of steps from the road, and felt a strange impulse to walk out in front of it. I had taken one step towards the road and then heard my husband's voice scream out, "Chris, get back!" His voice seemed to echo, but I stepped back, and as I did, whoever was driving the lorry held their hand on the horn. My body shuddered with the force and the power of the lorry as it passed by me. Alfie was instantly by my side, and he asked me why on earth I'd stood that close to the road. I said that I hadn't realised how close I was, and he pulled me back, away from the traffic.

My husband started to plant our trees, and the lady that lived in the farm next to the road came to see us. She asked how we were, and seemed very concerned for us. After we had planted our trees and made sure the one my mum had given us was planted, the lady brought water from the farm and told us she would keep them watered for us. The chimes my husband had hung up were still there, and every time a car went by you could hear them ringing softly. I had a set of chimes hanging on my bedroom window at home, and at the cemetery, and every time I heard them I always thought my Naylor was trying to tell me something. I know it sounds crazy and perhaps it is, but it was just something I had in my mind. I needed to think of it in the same way that I was still waiting for him.

I lit our candle and although I had in my mind that a candle burning would keep a spirit near, there was a deeper feeling; a light left burning and there was a door always open. Maybe I was waiting for Naylor, or maybe he was waiting for me, but in my heart, our two hearts beat as one. I laid some flowers next to the little angel, and although I always felt I needed to go back to this place, it was a strange feeling being there. As I am writing this paragraph I am looking out of my window. It is the 10th April , Six days before my son Naylor's Thirty Six Birthday so it's been ten years since we lost or son. The weather has been really cold, but I've just noticed that my magnolia tree has started to bloom. How strange, but beautiful. Little things like this means so much to me.

As we travelled home, I thought of how close the incident with the lorry had been, but Alfie and I didn't mention it. I think we both knew it would have ended up in an argument, and we were both too hurt for that. I glanced at my husband as he was driving home, and I could see the pain etched in his face, but it seemed that all he was concerned about was if I was all right, and I couldn't reach out and help him. We met the rest of the family back at the cemetery. It was now nearly evening, so after a while we lit our candle and returned home. I was carrying an empty feeling.

By now, there was always family in and out of our house all day, and I was never left on my own, and in the evenings, someone would pop in to see us, but we were alone at night and this last couple of weeks was the first time I had gone back to sleeping upstairs. Before I lost my son, Naylor, when my grandchildren stayed over, after bath-time I would always watch their favourite video with them before they went to sleep, and the one we had been watching was The Sword in the Stone. Every night, even though it was just me and my husband, I would have to put the video of Sword in the Stone on; I never watched it, just closed my eyes and listened to the story, but in some strange way it gave me a feeling of comfort. It seemed to take me back to when everything was all right. This was to become another ritual in my life.

So, my husband was the one trying to deal with the panic and fear attacks. They were still really bad and not one night could my husband get to sleep without me screaming out. I'd wake up screaming for Naylor, shaking like a leaf, and be wringing wet with sweat. It would be the same nightmares every time. I just kept reliving the first time I saw Naylor after the accident, when I tried to cradle his poor head, and I could still see blood on my hand. Or I would think I was at the scene of the accident, and I could see it so clearly. Some nights I would end up on the landing of our stairs, on the floor, lying there not even remembering how I had got there, but screaming for help.

My heart beat so fast that it was like having a heart attack. My husband would wake up and tell me it was just a nightmare, but I still believed I was there and beg him to help me. Most of the time, Alfie would end up with his arm around me, trying to keep me calm, and the saddest thing is that he would end up in tears with me, holding me until I went off to sleep. I know now this must have torn him apart.

I started to ask for more tablets. My husband still held them but he knew the attacks were still bad and getting no better. I'd started drinking more alcohol, as well, and Alfie told me that it was getting too much, but I didn't care so long as I could cushion the pain and sleep for a while.

CHAPTER EIGHTTEEN

SLIPPED BACK IN TIME

I really seemed to hit rock bottom after Naylor's birthday. One day, sitting in my back conservatory, I kept looking at my back door because I always had this feeling of waiting, and I couldn't get it through my head that Naylor wasn't coming home. I had a bad day and I was so upset; all I wanted was my boy. I can't remember much of what happened but I've been told by my husband that I'd had said that my two boys were playing and I could see them - it seemed as if I'd slipped back in time. Alfie has since told me that it was like I had a meltdown, so my mum was sent for, and the rest of the family. I had been so bad that Alfie was frightened to take me to hospital, so he decided to take me to a private doctor.

My mum and some of our family came along, and once there, my husband and my mum took me in. It was a private house and we were sitting in an office whilst Alfie spoke to the doctor, when my mum spotted a cat that had strolled into the room. Mum knew that I had a cat phobia and in normal times I would have jumped up and had to get out of the room, but she told me that I just sat and watched the cat walk toward me and brush itself around my legs. I can tell you now, if I had realised I would have been out of there like a shot, but my poor mum sat and watched in amazement as I sat there, oblivious to anything going on around me. I only know what my mum and my family have told me. I don't know what happened that day, or how my mind seemed to slip back and get stuck in the past.

After we had got home, I slept for a while and then I was back to how I'd been before and was soon asking my husband to take me to visit our son's grave, and lighting my candles. When my husband spoke to me about the attacks I could never remember. My mum spoke to me about the memory lapse. She thought it had all become too much for me and that I couldn't live in the present, it was too painful, so I must have blocked it out and gone back to a place in my mind when I was happy.

After I'd been checked over, the family was told that I needed counselling. They already knew I'd had a breakdown months back and were nursing me through it as best they could, and it was now obvious that if I had gone to my own doctor, or the hospital that had my records, I would have been sectioned. After that day, my husband really thought I had lost my mind. I would just sit and go back through Naylor's life, one step at a time, trying to remember the good memories; but I was still taking tablets and drinking at night, trying to get through this nightmare.

My husband arranged for me to see a private psychiatrist because he was so worried about me going to the clinic at the hospital. The psychiatrist I went to see was a very pleasant woman. I told her about my attacks and she talked me through all the different stages of grief as we talked about what had happened to Naylor. I wanted her help, and I listened to her every word, but when I left her house I didn't feel that anything was different; I was still dying inside. I had another appointment with her the following week and it went about the same as the first one, but I was still willing to try anything to stop the pain. In the meantime, my mum had to go back to the hospital because she had become very ill. Even though I was still getting the panic attacks and I wasn't really any help, I went along with my sister Charmain to take our mum to see the doctor because it was my place to do so.

By this time, cancer had hit my mum badly. I sat and listened to the doctors, but nothing seemed to sink in. My mind was like a sponge; it would absorb everything, but then it seemed that it just stayed there, and when my mum had to be examined I had to walk out and stand outside the door. I was no good to anyone really, just shaking and trembling with fear. I had lost my nerve and couldn't cope with what was going on. I left my sister to deal with the doctors, but it was my place to try to be there for my mum, and she always said that she knew I was just outside the door.

Things were going downhill with my mum's health. Both me and my sister were told before Christmas that it would be the last one we would have with her, but in my mind, I couldn't deal with it and tried to block it out. I know my mum knew she was dying; she was old school, and had seen too much throughout her years not to know what was going on, but it seemed that we were hiding it from each other. It was so sad.

I had noticed that my mum didn't call round to my house so often, and that's when I knew things were bad. One day, my sister picked me up to go to the hospital for an appointment for our mum, and as I got in the car, for the first time since I had lost Naylor, I noticed how poorly my mum looked. Normally, she would be the one asking if everything was all right, but today she seemed frail and weak.

As we arrived at the hospital, my sister parked in the front bays near the entrance, and then she and I helped Mum out of the car. She had a job to stand, and whilst my sister parked the car, I helped my mum to the door and she slumped up against the wall holding herself up as I was trying to help her. My mum was a strong woman and would never show it if she felt bad, but you could see the pain in her face. I walked in and told a nurse that my mum was very unwell and within a short time of waiting, our mum was taken into a medical room and a nurse helped her onto a bed. A doctor was called in and Mum was admitted to hospital straight away.

The doctor had asked Mum which pain-killers she was taking, and in her very polite voice when speaking to doctors, she told him, "Oh - just paracetamol". The doctor looked at my sister and me, and said, "This is one strong woman!" She was started on morphine straight away to help with the pain and the doctor said that he didn't know how she had managed to walk about at this stage of her illness.

Every morning, my sister picked me up from my house and we sat with our mum all day. Whilst we were at the hospital, a couple of the nurses picked up on me being unwell and became worried so they found time to sit and chat with me - they even offered to get me counselling. They knew my mum was dying and said it was a lot for me to deal with, having just lost my son, and now waiting for my mum to die, but inside, I knew my family was doing the best they could for me, and I told the nurses that I was already seeing a psychiatrist. When my mum was in hospital, her rest times were between 1pm and 3pm, so my sister and I would have to wait outside, and because I was still very ill myself, the nurses told us that we should go home so I could get some rest, too, but in our culture as Romanies we would sit all day with our mum and did not come home until we were told to leave, late evening.

My sister was very worried about me and tried to make sure that I did get some rest as well. She made me a bed by laying the front seat of the car right back, and I took my afternoon tablets and tried to rest my head, but it was nearly always the same; I would doze off and then wake up screaming in panic and shaking with fear. Sometimes, because we were in London, and right outside the hospital, there would be loud sirens making a lot of noise - maybe an ambulance or police car - and they would always set off alarm bells in my head, and I'd cower down, screaming for my sister to help me. I don't know how she coped; she would lay herself across me, holding me down until the shaking and fear had stopped, and this went on all the time my mum was in hospital.

My sister and I were told by the doctor that there was nothing else they could do for our mum. He knew we were Romanies and that we wanted to take her home to die, but he did want to tell our mum that there was nothing left that they could do. It became a bit of a task explaining to the doctor that we didn't want our mum to be told that, but the doctor was worried that she would want to put her affairs in order. We told the doctor that our mum knew that she was dying, but did not want to talk about it to us.

My husband has since told me that my mum spoke to him on his own. One evening, as he was taking her home from our house, she said, "I know I'm dying, Alf, but I don't want to talk about it to my gels. I don't want to hurt them." She was so concerned about me and said, "I want you to promise me, Alf, that you will take care of my Chris. I know she's not coping with losing Naylor. You make sure you look after her for me." My mum was sent home from hospital, and my sister and I told our family that our mum did not have long to live, so they all pulled together and made our mum as comfortable as they could. Mum was so ill that she couldn't come to my house any more so before my husband went to work, he would drop me off round at mum's house where she was living with my younger brother, Dean, and his wife, Zita, who was expecting their first baby. I was taking so many tablets by this time that I was out of it. I knew what was going on, but in my mind, I didn't want to know and life was getting worse by the day.

It was summer and our mum loved her garden. There were some beautiful standard rose bushes that our mum had planted and they were in full bloom, so when I was to sit with mum, I would always make sure that there was a beautiful rose on her bedroom windowsill and Mum always called me her flower girl. How I saw it was, my mum always took the time to buy me flowers, even though sometimes I might not have even noticed them. She was there for me, even though she was dying. It doesn't matter how old you are, there are times in your life when you need your mum, and this was the time I needed her most in my life, and now she had to leave me. I was dying inside, but nothing would come out. I was numb. By the time I arrived at mum's house in the mornings, she would already be out of bed and lying on a recliner chair that was in her bedroom. My sister used to stay at my brother's house to look after mum and when I walked into her room, the bed would already be made. I can hear her voice now. She would say, "Come on, my Chris. We got the bed ready for you and I want you to rest". I would lie on the bed and stay with my mum all day, and at this time I was on a lot of medication. Even though my mum was dying, she was still putting me first. One day, she told me that both of us needed a tonic because we were both so frail - she was a very old-fashioned woman.

The Macmillan nurses came every day. Mum had a photo of Naylor on her windowsill and she would tell the nurses all about him. My mum's younger brother Ambrose was dying with cancer at the same time and it was so sad listening to her saying, "I hope my Ambrose will be all right", because they were both so ill and both families were waiting for them to die - it was so hard. We had to translate their messages to each other on the phone. Once our mum was at home, it was like she'd had enough and couldn't go on. I still think that the shock of losing Naylor had finished my mum.

The family would be round every day, and they were living another nightmare. The end was near for our mum and the day came when the Macmillan nurses told us that they needed to fit a morphine box on her to control the pain. I felt like I was dreaming. I was still grieving for my son, and I didn't know what to do. At times, I was distraught and helpless, and all this time, my mum had made me lie on the bed and was still trying to look after me. Now the nurses told her that she needed to stay in her bed and Mum told them that she didn't want to, but the nurses insisted because they knew how ill she had become.

She was put in her bed for the last time and I stood at the foot as the nurses were sorting out the morphine box. Normally, I would have been out of the door if my mum needed anything done, but not this time. My mum needed me with her and so did my sister. Mum and I glanced at each other at the same time, and I had a churning feeling in my stomach. Our eyes seemed to fix both of us, each staring at the other. I will never forget that look in my mum's eyes; she seemed to reach deep into my soul with that long, last look at someone you love so much. I always worry how my mum felt that day, because we both

108

knew her life had come to an end, but we never spoke about it.

I knew how I was hurting for my son, and still carried the fear of him being hurt so badly, and me not being able to be with him when he needed me the most in his life, and here was my poor mum, who had been the most loving mum in the world, and she lay dying, staring at me. I knew she was leaving me through no fault of her own, and that I would be in this world without her at the most unbearable and distraught time of my life. Our lives had become so sad, and we needed each other as mother and daughter, both in the same situation, but in different directions. I will never forget that look on her face and it will stay with me forever.

After the nurses had left, Mum said she fancied something to eat so I sat with and tried to feed her, but she couldn't eat so we made her a cup of tea. She had a small mouthful and my sister and I sat on either side of our mum's bed, each holding one of her hands. She told us

Me, my Mum and Sister always together.

that she felt like going somewhere. In a low voice, she told us that my sister could pick her up, then she would come round and pick me up, and that we would stay together forever. She squeezed both our hands, her head was laid back on the pillow, and a teardrop trickled down her cheek. We both knew that it was her way of telling us that it was time for her to go.

A little while after, she slipped into a coma and never woke up. We sat with her, taking it in turns to hold her hand and as I took my turn during that night to sit and hold her hand, I sat watching her sleep and told her it was all right to let go of us, that we would be okay. I told her how much I loved her and thanked her for helping to take care of me, and told her what a wonderful mum she was. As I held her hand and kissed her face, I laid my head close to her and told her to sleep tight and that my Naylor and my dad would be waiting for her, and that I knew she would always be waiting for me.

I must have dozed off, because the next thing I knew I was on the floor. I'd had another panic attack and I couldn't even sit by my mum's deathbed without this nightmare destroying me. My sister, and Auntie Edie, who was our mum's sister who had been staying with us, were trying to sleep for a while but had been woken by my screams. My poor aunt was so worried because I couldn't stop shaking and although it was July she had to wrap me in a mourning coat and cover me with their blankets. The night was long and we sat until morning.

Our beautiful mum passed away early that day, with her family all around her. I didn't panic as I thought I would. I was there, but I couldn't cry out like I felt like doing; my body was just shaking with nerves. Her brother, Ambrose, had died two days before her - we never told her.

CHAPTER NINETEEN

GONE BACK IN TIME

The sitting up started again. Friends and family were in and out of the house, and it still didn't seem real to me. It was like I'd been dreaming. It had only been 11 months since I had lost my son, and my grief was still raw. It had overtaken my body and mind. Losing my mum at this time left me so disturbed that I just had a numb feeling, not knowing what to do. It was the same procedure as when we lost Naylor, the house being filled with family from all over, showing their respects.

As a Romany family, we bring our loved ones home and sit with them, and on the morning our mum was coming home, the family was standing outside, waiting, when my husband's phone rang. I heard him say, "Oh no!" and I could see there was something wrong. Then he told us there had been an accident, his cousin's son had been involved in it and had lost his life. We were all in shock and found it hard to take in. The young man who had died was Ricky, one of Naylor's best mates for years, and Naylor's best man when he got married. One of Naylor's other mates had died in the crash as well.

Naylor and friend Rick - Best man of Naylors wedding.

I told my husband that I would stay and wait for my mum to be brought home with the family and he went off to the hospital to be with his cousin, Tom, and his wife Debbie, who were Rick's parents. I remember thinking, 'not again' and my heart was with Debbie and Tom. We were all crying and very upset because another two young lives had gone. My nerves were shattered. I couldn't keep a limb still in my body and I asked my husband for my tablets before he left for the hospital. I told him I wasn't coping, so many people were talking to me and everything was echoing so loud, I said I needed to hold my own tablets, and that I knew what I was doing with them. I think Alfie was at breaking point himself by this time, and in shock he gave me the bottle of pills.

My mum was home for one night and as they laid her in the front room, all the family were in with her, paying their respects. I reached the door of the front room and looked over toward my mum. I could see her fair hair as she lay in the casket, and I turned around, walked away, and went upstairs. I locked myself in the toilet, shaking uncontrollably. Straight away I saw my son, as well as my mum, and

I had flashbacks of being taken to see my Naylor on the day of the accident. It had thrown me into turmoil and I could hear my Naylor's voice calling me, echoing round and round in my head.

I was shaking badly, and my head was spinning, my body was in a cold sweat. The fear and the panic washed over my body like giant waves and I ran to the tap to wash my face because I felt like I was going to pass out. Then I remembered my tablets that my husband had given me, so I took them out of my pocket and swallowed two of them, even though I had already taken two a short time before.

I can remember going back downstairs and going outside. People were talking to me but it wasn't making any sense. Things were fuzzy and in slow motion. I made my way back to the front room, stood in the doorway and looked over at my mum as she lay in a casket. I walked in and stood, just staring at her, still feeling numb. My poor mum looked just like she had always done. She had been a very smart woman for her age. I remember thinking, 'Oh, my God! Another one of my family has gone', and I had this fear that overwhelmed my body.

My husband came home from the hospital. After hearing how Ricky had lost his life in a car accident, he was devastated and we both felt so much sorrow for his parents, knowing the pain they would be facing. It was so sad for Ricky, who had lost his life so young, and for his three young sons and their mother. All their lives would be changed forever.

The night passed, the morning came, and my mum was leaving us forever. I can remember feeling sick with nerves, but it wasn't just about me. All my family loved our mum so dearly and although she had been so ill she had always seemed to be there for us all. It was so sad. My younger brother Dean's wife, Zita, was expecting their first baby and my mum had waited years for my young brother to become a father. My head was churning with thoughts. In our Romany culture, our parents always paid for our first newborns pram, but my mum was too ill to go shopping with my brother so she gave him the money to buy their baby's pram and although we were waiting for my mum's funeral to start, my mind wandered back. It is against our belief as Romanies to bring our baby's pram home before the child is born and safely home. One day, my mum and sister and me were sitting in our mum's bedroom when we heard my brother shout with excitement. "Can I come up?"

We knew he had gone out shopping for the baby because it was due any day, and we were all praying it would be before our mum passed away. I heard him striding up the stairs and I could hear the excitement in his voice as he came into the bedroom. He was holding the top half of his newborn's pram and he laid it on our mum's bed.

The look on our mum's face said it all. It was a look of contentment and pride as she ran her old, worn-out hands over the pram and told my brother and sister-in-law, Zita, how lovely it was. I was choking back the tears, as was the rest of my family. Our mum was talking to us and saying how much she loved the colour and that she knew the newborn would be beautiful. My brother had overlooked the old superstition of not buying a pram before the baby was born, just to let our mum see it. Then I came back to reality, and the horrible day that had dawned. I watched as my mum was carried out of her front door for the last time and I felt so numb. I can remember taking more tablets - it was the only way I could cope.

Once at the graveside, everything seemed distant and I felt so alone. I can remember feeling frightened of life; it felt like people I knew and loved were dying all around me and I wanted to cry, but I couldn't. Inside I was screaming out for help. I was trapped in this hollow and empty body. My mum was buried with my dad and my son. Naylor's grave is right alongside theirs and although my belief in God was shattered by now, in my head I was praying and asking Him to take care of them all. I felt so mixed up.

Dean and Zita's baby daughter was born the day after my mum's funeral and although we were all so pleased that the newborn was here, and everything was all right, and the baby was beautiful, just as my mum predicted, there was a sadness that overwhelmed the happiness of our family. We knew how hard it was for our young brother to bury his mum on the Friday and their baby to be born on the Saturday.

After my mum's funeral things became worse for me. I was taking more tablets and I started drinking more. Before my mum had passed away, I'd been seeing a psychiatrist, but how I felt now I couldn't see any point. It felt like there was nothing and nobody that could help me out of this misery I was living in. The family still came to stay with me whilst my husband tried to work, although from the day my husband gave me my tablets to hold for myself, I refused to let anyone else hold them for me. I felt safe because my tablets became a quick fix to help ease the pain.

I know I was taking more tablets than I should, but it was my only way of coping because the panic attacks were getting worse. Night-time was my enemy; I couldn't seem to go through one night without the dreadful attacks of fear and screaming out to wake my husband. He told me I was talking and begging in my sleep for someone to help me to get my baby back. There seemed no end to this nightmare I was living.

As soon as my mum's funeral was over, the sitting up started for my Uncle Ambrose and it was hard for both our families with one funeral after the other. Then there was Rick's funeral; he was buried in the same cemetery as my son, just a few yards from Naylor's graveside. It was so sad to see two young men who had been friends for so long, and to have lost their lives, so close together.

It seemed that every time we went to visit our son's grave, Tom and Debbie, Rick's mum and dad were always visiting their son's grave. It felt like I was in a dream, there seemed so much misery and despair in my life.

Just a few weeks after my mum's funeral came another hurdle of pain and turmoil. It was the eighth of August, 2004, a year since we'd lost our Naylor and all the family met at the graveside in the morning. My husband put up a gazebo over our son's grave because so many family and friends had brought flowers and came to remember Naylor. It was overwhelming, and the trauma of that day never left me throughout the year.

The same rituals were carried out; my husband and I laid flowers at the place where our son had lost his life and by now, on the long journey there, I knew how ill it would make me feel and the state I would be in, and I was sick of hearing my husband telling me to hold myself together. I missed my beautiful boy so much, and the pain and hurt I was feeling was unbearable, but I'd learned how to get my head on a level without the big screaming fits with my husband.

As soon as we left the cemetery, I would suggest that perhaps we should stop and get something to eat and drink before we set off. Once we'd stopped, my husband would ask what I wanted and my answer was always the same, "I'm not that hungry. I'll have a glass of wine", and it would end up being two or three glasses. Alfie would say, "You don't really need that amount," but I think our lives had got to a point where it became easier for each of us to do what got us through a bad day. My husband didn't know just how many tablets I was taking. I would take two or three tablets with my wine, even though it never did take away the pain, or my thoughts. It just mellowed my mind out so I became calmer. The homeward journey was in silence.

SELF-DESTRUCT

It became easy to get my tablets because I was seeing a private doctor, as well as my own GP and it became normal now to drink every night and pop more pills. As the months passed, I still wasn't coping, but the drink and the pills were getting me through each day as it came. I know this is weird, but I hadn't made a cup of tea or made myself anything to eat since I had the breakdown. My husband, or one of the family would always do it for me. I just couldn't be bothered to feed myself and I'd sit all day with nothing, but one morning after getting up, I walked downstairs straight into the kitchen and got three cups out of the cupboard. It was done without thinking, but there was a cup each for me and my husband and one for our son, Naylor. He used to call round most mornings for a cup of tea and breakfast, and I cried to myself as I put the extra cup back in the cupboard.

I remember getting a small bowl and putting cereal in it, and then realising how strange it felt to make a cup of tea and a bowl of cereal for myself. It was something I had done throughout my life, but it felt like the first time. I thought how pleased my husband would be so I shouted for him and, like a child doing something for the first time, I handed him his cup of tea.

We walked into the conservatory and sat down and as I took a mouthful of my food I told him, to my own amazement, to look at me; I was eating on my own and it was the first time without someone having to beg me to eat. Alfie stared at me and then stood up and walked away crying. It had been a strange feeling for me, but it must have been so hard for him to know that deep inside of his messed-up and disturbed wife there was this small part of me still there. That was the beginning of the first steps toward normality. After a while, I told my husband that we didn't need the family round every day, and I told him again I was sick of being baby-sat.

As the months passed, the family all started to try to get back to their normal lives. Our eldest son, Alfie, and our daughter, Phyllis, and all our grandchildren were trying to rebuild their lives. One day, my sisters-in-law came on a short drive with me to see how I was at driving, and because I was popping so many pills, I wasn't such a wreck when driving, but I can remember the fear on their faces that day.

All I wanted was to visit my Naylor's graveside without anyone else with me, and as time went on, my husband allowed me to drive myself. I would get up in the morning and visit my son's grave first thing. If my Naylor couldn't come to me, then I made sure that I could always go and sit with him at his graveside. Everything was still becoming ritualistic to me and that was one of my most important rituals, along with lighting a candle every night. I would often see Tom or Debbie at the cemetery when they were visiting their son's grave, as I was mine. We would chat about our boys and their children, and some days, I'd sit on my bench, looking across to Rick's grave and see

Debbie looking so sad. I knew the pain and hurt she was suffering as a mother having lost a son, but at this point in our lives, although we talked most days, we were too hurt to help each other. Life had become heavy and didn't have any meaning to it. It was very lonely for me.

All I wanted to do at this time was to wake up and for someone to tell me it had all been a dream, but that could never be. Since losing my mum, I still carried a horrible, numb feeling.

I thought back to the time when I had cut my wrist and the shame I had felt when my mum had seen me in such a distraught state. So, even though I felt like taking my own life most days, there was always a bit of me that knew I was hurting her. Out of respect for my mum, I'd tried to get through those bad days, but after losing her I had no need and I was slowly destroying myself day by day. The only time I seemed to get near normal was when my grandchildren came to stay, or my other children came to see me, but once they had gone that empty feeling was back.

I never let them know how I felt because I wanted them to get on with their lives, and it became very hard and yet normal to have a glass of wine in my hand nearly every time they saw me. All the family knew it was getting too much, but at this point they must have thought, 'Well, she is still here and getting through one day at a time', so as long as I wasn't put in the psychiatric unit, outwardly I was on the road to recovery, but inside I was far from it; I was on the road to self-destruction.

Some days, I would sit and look at the back door waiting for my Naylor to open it and shout, as he always did, "Where you at, my old gel?" One morning, I was upstairs when I heard Naylor call me and as I tried to get down the stairs, I slipped and fell halfway down them. My husband heard the bang and came running in and asked what had happened. I sat with my head in my hands, crying, and told him that I'd heard Naylor calling me. Alfie told me that I'd imagined it, but I just keep repeating, "No. I heard him. It was so clear." Whether I did hear Naylor, or it was in my head, I don't know.

On one occasion, I had wanted to buy Naylor's two boys some school shoes so I drove myself to a nearby town. I felt I wanted to do something myself for the boys and try to be a bit normal. My husband was worried because it was the first time that I'd gone to a crowded place on my own for so long. I told him not to worry and that I would ring him if I needed him. I got to the shoe shop and bought the boys' shoes, and was walking through the crowd when I saw a young man walk by me. He looked so much like my son that I watched him as he walked out of sight. I started to sweat and shake; it seemed that every young man who passed by me looked like my Naylor.

I was in a frenzy. I couldn't control my emotions and started crying as I felt the panic and fear running through my body. I had flashbacks and everything seemed so loud. A lady held onto my arm, asking if I was all right, and she had walked me to some stone steps that led to the car park. I don't know if it was the noise of the crowd, or what, but as the lady was speaking it was like in slow motion and I was only catching some of the things she was saying. She asked if I needed taking home and I told her I'd be all right and that I was going to ring my husband to pick me up.

Although I did ring Alfie and told him that I'd had a panic attack, and he was so worried that he told me to stay where I was and he would come and get me, I refused to let him. It had been the first time I'd been in a crowded place on my own, and I wanted to try to do something for myself. So he stayed on the end of the phone talking to me while I made my way back to the car and settled down. I sat in the car for a time. I'd taken some more pills to calm me down, and I thought, 'What a trauma it's become, just doing something so simple'. That's how my life was; I was living in hell. Time passed without me realising which month it was, except on occasions, and then I would come back to reality. I was locked in my own world.

CHAPTER TEWNTY ONE

GOODBYE TO MY OTHER CHILDREN

Months had passed since I had lost my mum. Most times on visiting the cemetery, although my son was laid to rest next to my mum and dad, and their graves were virtually touching, I would be so full of grief for my son that I would forget my mum and dad were there. Sometimes, I would get halfway down the path, walking out of the cemetery, and then think, 'Oh my God! I forgot my mum and dad'. I always walked back to kiss their gravestone and tell them I was sorry. I knew they would have understood.

One particular day, I really had such a bad attack and felt so low. It was so bad that I felt I wanted to take my own life. I'd been visiting my son's grave and I was so distraught and in a state, and then I looked over at my mum and dad's' grave and saw the pot where mum had always placed flowers for my dad. I missed her so much, but it was as if my feelings for my mum were locked away. There was no more room in my heart for any more pain, but on the way home, my mum was on my mind and I was thinking of all the times after losing my Naylor when she had tried to look after me, even when she was dying herself.

I walked into my house and for some reason my eyes glanced at the empty windowsill where my mum always placed a few flowers. It was her old-fashioned way of showing her love, and how much she cared, by taking the time to arrange flowers on my dad's grave. Now she was gone, and out of the blue, it hit me like a ton of bricks. I started to cry and couldn't stop. All this time, I had felt like stone and now, here I was, a mum and gran myself, sitting on the floor, rocking and crying for my mum. Once again, I found myself asking God for answers.

I don't know how long I had lain on the floor sobbing, but again, I reached for more pills and drink. I was still crying when Alfie came home, and for days afterwards. I was in a black place and I felt so low. From the time I had cut my wrist, I battled with a feeling deep inside. I felt that life was not worth living since losing my Naylor, but I would always try to pull myself up and think of who needed me, and the pain I would be putting them through again. I had pangs of guilt knowing how much pain I'd caused my mum when I had cut my wrist.

After I'd lost Naylor, Mum had told me that my life was going to be a hard journey and I needed to be strong for the rest of my family. She also told me that taking this path and staying on it would be the hardest task that I would ever have to do in life - and how right her words were; my mum knew how much my children meant to me and how I loved them unconditionally. All these thoughts and words were going round and round in my head, but I just couldn't pull myself up from this dark lonely place. Even though my mum was gone I would find myself talking to her, telling her I was trying to do what she'd told me.

It got to the point where I always seemed to end up hurting myself. It's so hard for me to write this because I know my children will read it,especially my beautiful daughter who took the time to help take care of me and get me through so many bad days and seeing so much pain in her young life. I know it will hurt them. They'll think 'How did we not know this was going on?' but it is the same as anyone with problems - you learn to hide it. I would hit my head on a door or anything that was near me, and it was always the back or the side of my head so no one could see the bumps and bruises. It was always the thought of my Naylor being hurt so badly, and me as his mum not being able to help him or hold him, and I would bang my head until the fear had gone.

My beautiful Daughter got me through so many bad days.

Hurting myself became worse after losing my mum. There was one time when I went to the cemetery early one morning that I will always remember because it was so cold that my hands were freezing, and the tops of my fingers were white and numb with cold. I pulled up and I'd been crying and felt so ill and low. I had my family around me, but the pain and the feelings of loss were getting worse. As I got out of the car, I put my hand in the door shut. I took a second and knew exactly what I was doing as I slammed the door on my own hand. I remember crying out, opening the door and walking down to my son's grave with my hand in my pocket, throbbing. My hand was bruised, but I told my husband that it had been an accident whilst getting flowers out of the car. Pain seemed to break the fear, but I know now, looking back, that it was because I couldn't get to my Naylor on the day of the accident. I would always get that flash of memory from when I had hurt my hand and he had run to me and wiped it with his T-shirt and kissed my hand - and here was my child, hurt, and I couldn't help him. It traumatised me and this time I just couldn't seem to pull myself up.

The depression and loneliness became so bad that I couldn't even go to Naylor's grave for a couple of days. I just lay all day where my husband left me in the morning and I'd still be there when he came home from work. He came in one day and asked me what I wanted to eat. I told him I'd already had something, but that was a lie. I hadn't eaten anything. Alfie told me that I needed to eat properly and to stop drinking, and this caused another argument between us. I told him that I couldn't go on like this. I wanted to die and be with my Naylor. I can remember him screaming at me saying, "What about the rest of your family? You've got to pull yourself together."

That night, my body ached with pain and grief, and I missed my Naylor so much, and could not cope. The panic attacks were so bad that my body felt like it was fading. I was sitting on the settee. I had been crying and Alfie said, "I think it's time you tried to get some sleep." I told him that I didn't want to go upstairs. I was lying on the settee and then I said, "I can't go on like this." I had stopped crying by this time, and told Alfie again that I couldn't go on anymore. He stood up and said, "You will never be at peace until you are with Naylor," and as he walked toward the stairs, he told me he couldn't see me like this. He said, "I've lost my son, and now I'm watching my wife slowly die. I don't think anyone will stop you doing what's in your mind. You've got your drink and drugs." He walked away crying, and told me that he loved me, but he would never forgive me for what was in my mind to do.

My husband went upstairs to bed and I sat and thought of my other children and how much I loved them and all the rest of the family. Then I thought of Naylor, and the day of the accident, and how badly he was hurt, and in my mind, I could still hear the coroner explaining the injuries and my mind was overwhelmed with thoughts. I was so depressed and in this dark place. I poured a large glass of neat vodka, emptied a load of pills into my hand, drank the vodka and took every pill. Then I drank the rest of the bottle, laid myself down on the settee and started to say my good-byes to my other children. I told them I was sorry for what I was doing. I was begging them for forgiveness as I felt myself drifting. My body felt heavy and I just lay there and gave myself up to die.

THE LORRY DRIVER

In the early hours, I felt my body being shaken and my husband repeating my name. He has told me since he sat with me nearly all day. I was so drugged that I couldn't lift my head from the settee, and couldn't speak without slurring. I must have slept all day. When I did come round to myself a bit, Alfie was sitting in the armchair and he said, "You must know by now that you are not meant to die. Look what you've taken!" The empty vodka and pill bottles were on the side. "Do you understand now? Naylor wouldn't want you to die." I wasn't taken to hospital. Alfie was at breaking point himself, and didn't know which way to turn next, but I know in my heart that if I were meant to die that day, he had prepared himself to let me go and be with our son, Naylor.

I lay there for two days, just sleeping on and off. The depression was still there, and the panic and fear were as bad as ever, and I had a heavy headache and hurt all over. I didn't know if I'd hurt my head banging it on the door, or whether it was the after-effects of the overdose on drink and drugs, but I felt so ill.

A few days later all I wanted was to go to my son's graveside. I took my pills and started my usual journey to the cemetery. I approached a roundabout and waited for a lorry coming from the offside to stop. It was so big that it came over the line a bit, and the man put his hand up at me telling me to stop, although it should have been my right of way. I flipped and was so upset that I was shouting something at the man, but I let him go first and as I followed the lorry, I was ranting and raving and upset. We got a few miles down the road and came to a set of traffic lights, where the lorry stopped in a different lane to me. I was behind other cars, and as I waited for the lights to change, the lorry driver put his head out of his window and looked back at me. Before I knew what I was doing, I was out of the car and running to the lorry driver, screaming at him, and asking what his problem was.

I brought all the traffic to a standstill. The lorry driver was in shock, and I will never forget his words to me. I felt so aggressive and I wanted to take my anger out on someone. I was upset with the world because I was still living and my boy had lost his life so young. I was repeatedly saying, "What is your f----- problem?" The lorry driver didn't shout or swear at me, he just said, "Look, luv. You're the one with the problem. You want to go home and have a good look at yourself. You have a big problem." The lights changed and he drove off leaving me standing in the road, holding up all the other traffic. Drivers were honking their horns, but I just screamed at them and then drove off. Once at the cemetery, I sat and cried, and thought about how bad I had been, and nobody had really done anything wrong - it was me.

When I returned home, I walked upstairs and did as the lorry driver said. I looked in the mirror and as I stared, I was horrified at how I looked. My eyes were black and they'd sunk right back in my head, and my skin was ash colour. My hair was so greasy it was flat to my head, and my clothes were hanging off me because I'd lost so much weight. I know I was ill, but I looked dreadful and was sickening to look at.

I was crying thinking how the lorry driver must have thought I was an alcoholic or a drug addict. He couldn't see that my heart was broken and I was dying inside, and that my anger was me crying out for help and all I wanted was my baby back. Then I thought, 'Why am I worried what a stranger thinks of me?' Suddenly, it hit me. What the lorry driver thought I was, I'd become. Through the grief of losing my son I had become an alcoholic and a drug addict. It was the only thing that could help numb the pain and get me through, one day at a time.

My life spiralled downhill so fast and as soon as I felt the fear and panic attacks come on I took pills and drank until I blacked out. It became too much for my husband and family to deal with. On a few occasions, it was so bad that Alfie thought I had died and he'd had no choice but to get me to hospital. Sometimes, I ended up staying in hospital and then went through the process of having to be kept in overnight and waiting to see a psychiatrist to help sort my head out, but Alfie always stepped in and said he would look after me, and do everything he could to keep me from being admitted in a clinic.

I had psychiatric nurses doing home visits, and had to attend a clinic every week to see a counsellor and a psychiatrist. I was told many things and asked a lot of questions, but nothing seemed to help. A few things stick in my mind from the sessions I had. I was told that I needed to go to the cemetery to say goodbye to my son. Once I had done this, I'd be able to move on. They told me that was why I always seemed to go back to the accident. At this time in my life, I would have tried anything to escape this nightmare I was living.

I went to the cemetery and remember standing there, crying and looking at my son's grave. I was thinking, 'How do I do this?' I was in such a state, and in the end, I was on my knees telling my son that I was sorry even for thinking of saying a final goodbye. There is no goodbye. I knew this was wrong. How does a mother say a final goodbye to her child and let go forever? I couldn't do it. I spoke briefly to my daughter about it and she felt the same. She said, "If you say goodbye it's final, and he will be gone forever." She was so distressed. Whilst having this chat, she also told me that she could not stand the thought of me being sectioned, put in a clinic and ending up not even remembering why I was there in the first place. She told me that she'd rather see me go with Naylor and if this was to be the final result, then she would give me the pills to do it. It makes me sad to know that my daughter was put in this position, to think that there was no return for me in her young mind. This is the fear that stems from the old Romanies and their view of mental health problems, no matter the reason that you have them. Once you're involved with psychiatrists, you're going to be locked up and never come out. This was the fear my husband and family were living with; to them, dealing with mental health was the unknown. In no way were my family ignorant of the fact that the clinics and the doctors were there to help. It was the circumstances they were facing. Their thoughts were, 'How do you mend a broken heart, and find someone who's lost and still waiting for someone to walk back through the door, knowing that it was never going to happen?' The only thing in their eyes was love and being with my family, not locked away in a clinic.

One psychiatrist, at every session, asked why I was wearing black clothes and I told her that I had recently lost my mother. It was to show respect, in my Romany culture, to do so for the first year. I was told to wear something bright on the next visit, but I told her that I couldn't do that. It didn't help when someone was trying to change your beliefs, and another thing that was really upsetting was that they talked about Naylor as if they knew him.

There was a time when I was talking to a psychiatrist about the day of the accident and this one thought stuck clearly in my mind. I knew Naylor was hurt so badly, and in my mind, I could hear him, and see him asking someone to get his mum for him. There were times throughout Naylor's life, even after he was married and had children of his own; maybe when he had been out with his mates or even at work with his dad, if he had felt unwell he would nearly always ask to be brought home to me at my house. It might have been something as simple as the flu or toothache, but Naylor knew I was always there to help him and look after him, even if it was me taking a trip to the chemist to buy remedies to take home with him. So, the thought of him lying there that day, and asking for me, haunted me even though I was told by people who had tried to save my son that he had died instantly. The very idea of not being able to help him and hold him was destroying me, and having to tell a psychiatrist this, and then having her tell me that she knew Naylor wouldn't want me to think like this, but she didn't know him, and throughout this conversation, her every other word was, "I know Naylor.." In my mind, the words were rolling round, '...but you didn't know Naylor', and I knew in my heart that he needed me. I knew they were trying to help, but they really weren't.

As the time passed, I couldn't seem to talk to any of my family about Naylor or how I was feeling, because it was tearing them apart and they would always break down and start crying, so I found a way of unloading my troubled mind without even realising myself at the time. I could have gone to the doctors, or to the cemetery... anywhere ... I always seemed to find someone to start a conversation with and looking back, it may have been the way I looked. Perhaps I looked desperate, I don't know. It was always strangers, but before I knew it I would start pouring my heart out about my Naylor. I'd start from how I lost him and tell them how much I loved him and missed him, and I'd always end up breaking down and crying, and I could hear in my own head that I was probably always over-talking, but I just couldn't stop myself from talking about Naylor.

I soon realised that when I was talking to strangers I could say whatever was on my mind and they could listen without breaking down, although on some occasions they would cry with me. We were crying together, but it didn't feel the same as when talking to my own family. They were always the ones in control, and if I said I was sorry for upsetting them, they would say, "Don't be silly. You're okay." and I felt I could go on talking and it was like someone was pulling a weight off me.

On the other hand, if it had been one of my family and they had started to cry and break down, I always felt guilty for making them relive something they would rather not. If I spoke to my husband, he would try to tell me that I had to be strong and think of my other children. It always ended the same, me screaming and saying that I couldn't. So, as sad as it may seem, strangers became my saviours, although there were times when it became a problem. If my daughter dropped me to the hairdressers, I would start talking about Naylor and then I knew I had to go back one day and felt ashamed for talking so much and breaking down. I would get embarrassed by this and make up an excuse so I didn't have to go back there. I often worried what they thought of me for not returning for my next appointment.

The family never knew this, along with a lot of other things I have gone through without telling them. It's strange though, seeing all sorts of people in the medical field that were trying to help me and not being able to open up my true feelings to them. I think that, along with my family, there was a fear of the unknown and although they were trying to help I felt frightened, and sometimes vulnerable, like I was going to say the wrong things and how I really felt about life.

When I was talking on the days when I felt that I wanted to end my own life, I wanted to tell them I didn't care what happened to me. Some days, I felt I wanted to be admitted to a clinic and never return home. I found everyday life so hard to deal with. There was always a little bit of me struggling with telling the truth, though, plus the thought of ending up in a clinic and my family having to deal with me being sectioned, apart from dealing with the stigma in our culture of them not being able to look after me, and deep down I knew this wasn't the Romany way. Until this day, with some of the elder Romanis, once you have been in the divvy kenner, and that would apply to mental health clinics, you can't detach yourself from the stigma.

MY BEAUTIFUL MIRAGE

Months and years rolled round, and I had more times down than up. The days I was up would be hypo and alert and I soon found that it was linked to when my grandchildren stayed at weekends. I only realised that when I hit rock bottom as soon as they had gone home. Throughout my illness, Naylor's two young boys still stayed every weekend and they loved to be with me.

Over time, I developed a way of taking myself to a place where I was happy before I lost my son. This beautiful place was a cottage by the sea. I'd close my eyes and imagine all my children and grandchildren around me. It was a warm summer day and we'd all arrived for a holiday. We were always a very busy family, and in this beautiful image, my husband and my eldest son, Alfie, would be cooking on the barbecue; they both loved cooking for their families, and my son-law, Billy, would be sorting out the fishing gear for after lunch. My daughter, Phyllis, and daughter-in-law, Rosy, would be sorting out the children and getting the dinner table ready. Then I would hear my phone ring and then, "I won't be long, my old gel. I'm just up the road, not too far away." My Naylor was always late arriving, and I was always waiting for him.

In my happy place, I am standing and looking down because the cottage is high up in a beautiful green pasture, looking over the sea, and in my mind, I can hear the waves hitting the rocks below. As I look down the long path that leads down to the road, and the village below, I can see my Naylor and his family in the distance. As they get closer, I can see Naylor with his youngest son, Razzo, on his shoulders, holding his little legs with one hand, and holding his elder son, Naylor's hand with the other, and his wife Sue walking next to him. I always scream back to the others, "Naylor's here!" and then I run down the path to get to him. I cuddle him so tight and I don't want to let him go. He smiles at me with that shy smile he's had from a child. We walk to the cottage and join the rest of the family and spend a beautiful day together eating, laughing, children playing.

Only thinking of this place with Naylor there makes my heart miss a beat. I get the warm glow of a mother's love running through my body and I don't want it to end. It's become a sanctuary for me, even though I know I've captured precious moments from my life and stored them without even thinking.

It seems the picture I have of Naylor with his two young boys comes from when we spent his last birthday together in the park. I have created an image from all the things that I've seen and lived before, but the waiting feeling comes from now. I'm waiting for my Naylor. It could be that he waits for me, though - who knows?

No one ever told me to create this place in my mind. I found it on my own in my darkest hours, and some might think it's wrong, but I know my imaginary vision has pulled me up when I've been down so low, and given me peace and allowed me to live another day. Over the years, I have taken many paths to find peace in my mind from those panic and fear attacks, trying to find light in my darkest days, including trying to believe in so many different religions.

I say 'trying' because after losing my son, what belief had was torn away and somehow I was left in limbo with nothing. Even all the beliefs that I had been brought up with as a little girl were gone, so I would push myself to believe in something, but every time I would hit a wall. Why my Naylor, God? Why not me instead? I just could not get my head around it, and I'd get into a different religion than my own, grabbing for anything. I found myself talking to people about their beliefs and I can honestly say that I would never criticise them, even when I hit the wall of disbelief. Everyone has the right to their own opinions, whatever they are.

There is one thing that I still believe in, though. Something handed down to a young child from older people in the family, and that is the white feather; there is a saying, whenever a white feather appears, an angel is near. On several occasions after losing my Naylor, I'd

Picture taken by P.J. Gathergood

come across a white feather and I would always get a strong feeling that Naylor was with me. I found a lot of comfort in it because they always seemed to appear so unexpectedly, but looking back, it was always at my lowest points.

One time that sticks in in my mind, strongly. It was when I thought of writing this book. I had talked it through with my good friend, Terry, and close family, who all told me it would be very hard to do, but I told them I had so much in my head, and in my heart, that all I needed to do was put it on paper.

My first step was to tackle a computer. I couldn't even turn one on, so my grandson, Naylor, daughter, Phyllis, and my husband Alfie, went

133

out and brought me my very own computer. After a few lessons, and a lot of patience from Naylor, I opened the first page, and soon found that going over that unbearable day when I lost my son, although I had done so many times before, and writing it down was like reliving it all over. It was not going to be as straightforward as I'd thought.

I soon come to a block and just sat staring at the screen. I sat there for what seemed hours and then decided to leave the laptop open and make myself a cup of tea. I walked back into the room, thinking that I'd been told how hard this was going to be, and there was so much doubt in my mind whether or not to carry on. Then, as I sat down next to the computer, I glanced over and saw a perfect white feather lying on the keys and felt a wonderful glow of love for my beautiful son. I felt that Naylor was with me. I cried, told him that I missed him and how much I loved him, sorted myself out, picked up the computer and started typing.

I wrote so much that day. It was like I said, when a white feather appears your angel is near and I will always believe it. Alfie believes it too, and it brings us comfort. Looking back, it has happened at times when I've been at my lowest, but for some reason that one time stands out in my mind.

Looking back through my time of grief, there was always a reason, even when I had hit rock bottom - and there were more times down than up - that I fought my way back without realising it. Knowing that Naylor lost his beautiful life so young, and having so much to live for, did not only affect me as his mum, but it also tore our family in different directions, all dealing with their own grief. Every one of them, including Naylor's dad, and close friends as well as his family, plus his two children, were dealing with their grief in different ways. I found that no two people grieve in the same way. My two other children's lives were in turmoil, there were times as their mum when I just wanted to put my arms around them and take away their pain, but I was in a bubble and couldn't reach out. My husband, Alfie, was carrying me, as well as himself. One day, after he had gone off to work, the phone rang a few hours later and he was calling to ask if I knew which job he should have been at; I could hear he was crying. He told me that his mind had gone blank and he couldn't cope. He missed our son so much, and he was the one trying to stay strong for all of us. Grief can take the strongest person down, and even though Alfie thought he was coping, he clearly wasn't. His business went bankrupt, and some people think that it must have been a way to get out of a bad business, but it wasn't. My husband had a good business and it was doing well, but it got so that he couldn't even measure a job up without getting it wrong. It had all become too much for him and he could not cope. He was sitting in a chair one day and looked like he'd had a stroke. It was Bell's Palsy, and I now know that's when his grief really hit him. He had been too busy taking care of everyone else.

As time passed, even though I was ill, I noticed that Naylor's oldest son, Naylor, wasn't dealing with his grief. I couldn't deal with my own life, but I made sure that Naylor's two young boys stayed over, because they loved to be with me, and their granddad. Their bath times always seemed to be our time to talk. We would fill the bath with loads of bubbles and the two little boys would splash about playing, like children do, and while watching them play, I would always ask how they were doing at school and ask how things were at home. I also told them that if they had any problems, or needed to talk, they always knew I was there.

Razzo was my son's youngest. He had only been four years old when he lost his dad. Naylor was the eldest boy and he'd been six years old

at the time. Both boys would ask me about things that their dad had done; they loved to hear stories that included their dad as a little boy. It was as if they were worried that they might forget him, but I must have felt that with them because we made a memory book and wrote some of their memories down.

The boys were different in their ways. Naylor always seemed to get very sad when it came time to go home. There would always be tears, and as time passed he became unsettled at school. Razzo would get very angry and showed it through his tantrums. My husband, Alfie, got the boys into driving horses; it was a love we all shared because horses had always been a part of our lives. One day, one of the horses was playing up and I was holding the leading rein, when I felt someone pulling at me and as I turned and looked, I could see it was my

Naylor juniour. At the same splash as his dad swam in.

Out walking with their dad's dog Old Red.

grandson, Naylor. He was pulling me and telling me to let go of the horse, and then he cried out. "I don't want you to die and leave me, Gran!" I gave the lead to my husband and cuddled Naylor reassuring him that I was all right, but that day was a turning point in my life. It made me see so clearly that my little grandson, Naylor, was carrying so much pain inside, and was still so full of grief and frightened.

CHAPTER TWENTY FOUR

FIRST STEPS TO RECOVERY

As time passed, my son's wife, Sue, moved on with her life. My grandson, Naylor, became unsettled and soon after came to live with Alfie and me. The day he moved in with us, he was sitting on the settee in his school uniform and he had always been tall for his age, but that day he looked so small and I could see hurt in his eyes. That was the day I knew I had to sort myself out and take care of him. Here was a child who needed me, and little did I know that this was going to be part of my recovery, having to get up to prepare my grandson's breakfast and get him ready for school, helping him to do his homework, washing his clothes, taking care of him if he wasn't well - all the things you do without thinking as a mum, and all I had known was to take care of my children in the past.

There would be no more binge drinking for days, and taking drugs whenever I felt I wanted to get away from my traumatised life. I had a child in the house and needed to set an example. In no way was this easy. I didn't stop taking my medication, and I still had a few glasses of wine here and there, when my grandson was in bed. As I said, I'd become an alcoholic and was addicted to prescribed drugs, and that couldn't be changed overnight. It has got harder for me to admit, as time has gone by, and I get embarrassed by the things I said and did in my darkest days, but this book is based on the truth as I remember it, and that was the truth. I wanted to be strong for my grandson, Naylor. I wanted him to have a good life, a childhood he could look back on and be happy and feel content about, and to make his life better, so I couldn't cry whenever I felt like it, or sit around depressed for days, not doing anything. I still cried every day for my son, and was still depressed, but I was in control. I soon learned to cry in my own time, and my sitting and moping took a dramatic twist - I kept myself busy because I found it hard to sit and relax.

All in all, my grandson had a good stable home, and we would help each other. I knew in a second when he was down, and I would always talk things through with him and tell him, all the time, "If you need to talk, you know I'm here."

As I said, everybody grieves in different ways. Naylor was a very quiet child, and even though we used to talk about his dad, he only asked about the accident his dad was in after a few years, and each time it was very briefly. I knew there were things he wanted to say, but couldn't and I know I was the one that he opened up to, but I didn't forget that he had seen me at my lowest, and used to feed me, along with my other grandchildren, when I had the breakdown and could not feed myself.

At the age of fourteen, Naylor wanted to do boxing so my husband took him to a boxing club where our sons once boxed, and he loved it. He won his first couple of fights and was doing well. Shortly after Christmas, Naylor had another fight coming up and he had his shorts made with 'Dad. Love you always' on the leg, and one of his dad's

138

Timberland boot laces tied inside. It was what he had chosen himself.

Once at the boxing show, everything seemed to be as normal. There were a lot of Romany men and plenty of my Naylor's friends who came to see his son box. Naylor got into the ring and was taking the first round and then the bell went, so each boy sat in his corner.

Our son Naylor, boxed for Slough.

My grandson Naylor wanted to box like his Dad.

Naylor came out in the second round and I knew something was wrong. He looked like he was stunned, and didn't even put his hands up to protect himself. The fight was stopped, but Naylor had two black eyes and looked dreadful. It was put down to him not being fit enough for the fight. Alfie told our grandson that he wanted him to finish with the boxing because he didn't want to see the boy hurt like that anymore.

Next morning, Naylor and I were alone and I knew something wasn't right. We sat and talked and he seemed distressed. First of all, he admitted that he wasn't as fit as he should have been. He told me that when he was sitting in his comer, waiting for the second round to start, he'd glanced down and seen the word 'Dad' on his shorts and his dad had been on his mind a lot that day. As he stood up to start

CHRISTINE BALL

the second round, all his friends, and his dad's friends were standing up, shouting him on. He went on to say that he thought he'd seen his dad, and heard him shout from the crowd, and after that he had felt stunned.

He became so upset whilst repeating to me, "...but me dad's not coming home, is he Gran?'" and then went on to tell me, for the first time, how on that dreadful day he had waited all day for his dad to come home to help fill up his swimming pool. He told me how his mum had told him that his dad wasn't coming home any more, and we spent all day crying and talking Together.

Although Naylor and I were very close and loved each other very dearly, and we could talk about almost anything, it had become clear that we were worried about hurting each other by going back too deep over that dreadful day. Naylor had locked that day away in his mind, but now he needed to talk about it.

I asked my grandson how he felt about his boxing and after we'd talked, he told me he loved the sport and wanted to carry on, and as I looked at his bruised face, my heart ached. I told him that if it were me, I would carry on and not let it beat me. As painful as it was for me to tell him to go on, deep down I just wanted to protect him. I didn't ever want to see him hurt in the ring again, but I knew if he let his grief stop him doing something he loved, it could destroy his life. I wrote this chapter hoping that it might bring some light and help anyone in a similar situation. It shows if your mind and body are exhausted, and Naylor wasn't fit, grief can take you to your lowest ebb and destroy you and all you believe in.

Naylor went on with his boxing. He is dedicated to his training and he has gone on to win more fights - in 2013 he won a silver medal and 2014 he won gold. He's also training to be a personal trainer and is in the up-and-coming

He's a winner and for many reasons.

young talent squad for the GB team. I am so proud of him.

Over the years, I have always tried to be there for my son's two boys, even though my grandson, Razzo, was only four when his dad died, he has not gone without his problems. He had a bit of upset at home one day, normal everyday things that you would expect from a fourteen-year-old and he came over to see me that afternoon. I could tell by the look on his face that he needed to talk, and we sat there he told me he found it hard to remember things about his dad. It made him angry and upset. I told him how much his dad had loved him, how his dad always picked him up and put him on his shoulders and reassured him, and how proud his dad had been on the day he was born.

Grief appears in many ways. Growing up, Razzo has had to deal with holding on to just a handful of memories of his dad. He's had to rely on family to learn all about his dad, who he will always hold in his heart so dearly. Razzo has also become a strong and beautiful young man who I love very much. He is studying at college and is doing well, and he makes me feel so proud.

When I lost my son, Naylor, I could only cope with living in the past and I forgot how to live life. Looking back over

Razzo has had his own challenges, and he too has became a fine young man.

the years, there have been mixed emotions, with the sadness of our loss, and joy with the birth of three more grandchildren, and there are things that make me laugh now, but made me cry then. It was the first year that Naylor moved in with me and Alfie, and as I said earlier, things had to change. Christmas drew nearer, and Naylor said, "I'm going to buy you a Christmas tree, Gran."

It was going to be the first Christmas we had put a tree up, since losing our son. Part of me felt sad, like I was moving on, and it was the same feeling I used to have if someone made me laugh, like it was wrong for me to be happy, but once the tree was up and Naylor had finished decorating it and with lights and tinsel around the house, it brought a magical glow of happiness - even though we did look like the Griswalds. Naylor had put lights up around our archway and TV with black masking tape - not a pretty sight - but he was so delighted to be making me happy that I didn't have the heart to tell him we needed hooks.

Christmas Eve came, and we sat as a little family together, watching TV; grandson Naylor with all his treats and very excited, waiting to get his presents the next day. I decided that I wanted to go to midnight mass for the first time, and the local church was at the end of our road, about 300 yards away. It had snowed before Christmas and the ground was still very icy and snowy, and Alfie decided he didn't feel like going, so my grandson and I set off. Naylor was holding me by the arm. He's always been tall and I am only short, so I was taking three or four steps to his one stride. I was marched down the street and I can only describe it as a scene from the Quiet Man. We resembled John Wayne walking across the fields, dragging his wife behind him. I couldn't stop laughing.

I'd had a few glasses of wine throughout the evening, and as I said, I hadn't been drinking as much since Naylor lived with me, so once out in the fresh air I felt tipsy. We walked into the church and sat down, and we listened to the vicar talk, and then he said, "Let us pray" so I lowered my head, closed my eyes, and the next thing I knew was my grandson elbowing me and saying, "Gran! Wake up!" I must have dozed off. Naylor was giggling and I tried to make up with the singing, but I was out of tune and a bit loud so you can imagine the look in people's eyes, staring over the top of their hymn books.

I knew our local vicar well, so after the sermon I told my grandson that I wanted to light a candle. He looked at me in amazement and said, "Gran, the church is lit only by candlelight. I don't think they will have any left." I told him, "Don't worry. I need to say Happy Christmas to the vicar. I will ask him then." We finally got through the crowd of people and arrived to where the vicar was standing. I blurted out, "Hello, vicar. I'm sorry, but I'm a bit drunk." His reply was, "Oh well, Christine. Not to worry," with a little smirk and giggle. "At least, you're honest, and you're here." Then he rallied round and had someone find me a candle to light so I could say a prayer for my son.

On the way home, Naylor couldn't stop laughing and he told me that when I'd fallen asleep I was snoring, and he showed me how awful I was at singing. There was no way my singing was as bad as he was impersonating me. It was a Christmas we will always remember, and it always makes us laugh.

As life passes and time goes by, I still live day-by-day, and it surprises me how the simplest of things can change my feelings, like an overnight stay at Weymouth, in Dorset. I was there with family and watching my grandchildren playing on the beach; a couple of my grandsons were on a small boat. The sun was shining and it was so hot, the perfect day, with everything I loved, sitting and watching my family. I was looking at the most beautiful scenery, a clear blue sky and cliffs all around, and it was serene. Then an overwhelming realisation of the life that my son had lost hit me so hard. My dad's words went round in my head, when he told me that his sunshine had been taken away.

I felt my body shake and couldn't stop the tears from flowing. I knew then that life was too good to let go. The pain of my son losing his life so young haunted me, and this had happened to me so many times before, but this time, instead of reaching for the bottle or taking pills to help with the pain, I took control of my life and jumped straight up, ran toward my grandchildren, and joined in with what they were doing. This was my learning curve. I now know that I can't sit and dwell on the times that have passed. I have got to be in control and push forward, even when it's harder to go forward than to go back.

CHAPTER TWENTY FIVE

EPILOGUE

Over the last thirteen years, it's like I have been on a long journey and my path has been so rocky that I have got lost and strayed from it in different directions. I've had to learn to channel my mind, and it began by talking. I found that I could talk to strangers more than my family. I used to talk to my daughter a lot, but sometimes I would go too deep into what happened to Naylor, and then see so much pain in her eyes. I didn't want to upset her, so I couldn't say the things that were killing me inside. The same applied to the rest of my family, but in the early days I couldn't talk to counsellors, and this was because of the fear in my Romany culture. I was frightened to tell them how I really felt, and looking back now, I know I would have been better off talking to them, but you get lost and frightened and things soon spiral out of your control.

As time went on, and after my grandson, Naylor, came to live with me, my life took a twist. Instead of just sitting and thinking, and trying to live in the past, I found that the more everyday family things I was able to do, the more I could cope; making jam, or other activities with the grandchildren, an interest in horses, dogs and so on - anything that would keep my brain on the right track, but it took so much strength.

When all my children were young, I went to college for floristry and so I started going back in that direction. My daughter and I designed flowers for weddings, funerals, any occasion, and I designed those pieces with so much love and care. It brought me close to people who had lost loved ones, the same as me, and I connected so easily. A man came to see us who had lost his son. He was in such a bad state and it brought so many memories flooding back, but I remember crying when he cried and then listened when he talked, because I knew this is what I would have wanted in my early days of grief. When it was time to choose the floral tributes for his son, and we spoke about the things his son loved in life, I took the time to help him to pick the tributes for his son's funeral. I didn't want him to have the regrets that I felt. I can't remember sorting flowers out for my son's funeral. I couldn't even remember seeing the flowers, only when a good friend of the family, Terry Doe, who had taken photos of Naylor's flower tributes and had taken the time and kindness to put them all in a photo album. It was a long time after I had lost my son that our friend, Terry, asked if Alfie and I would like to see the pictures. I remember feeling very nervous, but the first time I saw those pictures of my son's flower tributes, it made me realise how much people loved him, and the meaning of the personal tributes made me feel proud that he had so many good friends and family who loved him so much, and will always remember him.

I regret that there are still so many blank parts in my mind. I'm not able to remember certain things after I lost my Naylor, even though that is no fault of my own, really. I just couldn't deal with it at the time. I still have to rely on my family and friends to fill in those blank spaces, and it was very frustrating when writing this book. I did speak to a doctor about my memory lapses and he seems to think that when something really bad happens in your life that you're not dealing with, your brain can shut it out.

I have tried to help a lot of people during the later years since losing Naylor. I feel so connected with people who have lost a child or a loved one. I suppose, if you have lived through it yourself, you know first-hand how they feel; you're not just reading text from a book.

Talking is the key tool to deal with grief when there is someone there to listen, and knowing you're not alone. These days I do a lot of talking. I work in the family business, a small sandwich shop that we called 'Naylor's'. It has become a lifeline for me. I know everyone who comes in and it brings me such joy and contentment just to hear someone in the queue make a call to a friend and say, "Hi, I'm at Naylor's. Would you like a sandwich?" Just hearing my son's name means so much to me.

If I have a sad day, I might mention it in conversation, and the customers will take time to talk with me and I know they care very much. It has been a therapy in itself, and it has worked both ways. If anyone comes in with everyday problems, I make sure that I take time to listen to them and it might not even be connected with losing someone. I have one young man who's had problems and suffers with depression. When he is down, he calls in for a chat and reassurance, and a hug, and that goes a long way, just to know that someone outside of the family cares and has got time to listen. It makes me feel good in myself that I am strong enough to be there when someone needs me. If any one comes in the shop for a sandwich perhaps they might not have enough money on them - there are times when we have all been in that situation - and if I am serving they never go without what they want. That's how I am, but you can be sure they always bring it in what they owe when they're passing Naylor's sandwich bar, and all the customers are like one big happy family.

There was a time when I was behind the counter and I noticed a man sitting in the corner with a cup of coffee. I could see at a glance that there was something wrong, so I walked over and asked him if he was all right. He started talking, and I could see the tears in his eyes and the pain on his face.

"I'm sorry," he said, "but I am having a bad day." Then he told me how he had lost two of his sons. He went on to tell me that whilst grieving for one of his sons, he had lost the other one, and as he told me how they died, I could feel my heart beating fast and thinking, 'How is he still standing?

He told me that he and his wife had turned to God after losing their sons and invited me to their church. I told him that I didn't feel I was ready for church, but maybe one day, I might. I told him how I admired their strength and the courage they had found. I so often think of them. They call into the shop now and then for a coffee. It's always nice to see them and have a chat. People have different views on life and deal with grief differently, and everyone is entitled to respect for their beliefs.

Things in my life have changed, but it doesn't mean I forget. I have still got my son Naylor's clothes hanging up in the wardrobe. I sleep with one of his T-shirts that he liked held to my chest at night. If I go on holiday, or stay away overnight, the first things I pack are a picture of Naylor and his T-shirt; they are a comfort to me. I have many things that I hold dear to me that belonged to my son, but this doesn't mean I'm not dealing with my grief.

I know some people who can't look at photos of their loved ones, and have to let go of all their belongings, but this doesn't mean they're wrong. Each person should deal with their grief in a way that brings them comfort. Looking back, it didn't seem right when counsellors told me to go to my son's grave and say goodbye. In my heart, there are no good-byes. Naylor will always be with me. I love him and he will always be my handsome young man as I saw him the last time in his life, but that's how I cope with my grief, knowing that he lives in my heart.

In the shop, during the day I have had so many of my son Naylor's friends call in and see me, and it's always good to see them, and so uplifting to know that his memory goes on. After looking through the photo album of my Naylor's flower tributes, there was one that stood out in my mind. One of my son's best mates had it made and it read, 'One of the Boys' and I know that's how his friends will always remember him. It brings me so much comfort to know this.

Always was, always will be.

I hope this book will help people who are going through the darkest days of their lives. I want them to know that you can get back from the nightmare, and that during the long journey, you have only lost sight of your family and life temporarily. You have got to be strong and talk to someone, and eventually, you will see the rest of your family. Just reach out and they will hold on to you and help you back from that dark, lonely place. When you're at the weakest time of your life, remember that you are who you are because of the love you shared with that person you loved so much.

My love for my husband, children and grandchildren will give me the strength to go on. Life's not easy. I miss my son, Naylor, and if you'd asked me five years ago how I felt, I would have told you that I could see no light. I really didn't care about my own wellbeing, but now I try to take care of myself because I know how my children and grandchildren rely on me; they need me and I am a big part in their lives.

I have written this book truly how I lived through it. There were some very distressing times that I went through in my grief for Naylor, and it's been hard to put my personal life in black and white for everyone to read. It's in my heart and my head, and I thought all I had to do was put it down on paper, but by doing that I have had to relive it - maybe

149

Rules: 7

it's helped me by getting it out.

It's been so hard. It's taken four years to write this book, but I stopped when it became too much, and restarted when I was able - and there was a time when I felt that I couldn't go on with it, but I learned to channel my mind and to be strong when I felt like giving up.

It's like, there I was; here I am. Love to me is from the beginning to eternity. My son, Naylor's love is always there. He lies on in my heart forever, even after death. Your loved ones are only gone if you let them go, and the art of living after losing someone is to live on the stars, and not beneath them. Your heart and soul will always be with them.

I will never forget the wonderful nine months of carrying my beautiful Naylor. I can close my eyes and remember resting my hand on my tummy, feeling our two hearts beat as one. That's a feeling that takes my breath away, and it will last forever, and that's where I felt I needed to end this book - at the beginning of my love for my son, with two hearts beating as one. My life will go on because his love keeps me strong.

Expecting Naylor. Two heart beats as one - and that's how it will always be.

"Here on earth it feels like everything good is missing since you le[ft] there's an emptiness. I hope the angels know"

THE LAST CHAPTER

ALFIE

As I write this last chapter, I am still in disbelief. When I started this book, I had no idea that I would have to write about the loss of my husband; My beautiful Alfie, my best friend, my rock, the love of my life, the one person who was by my side through my darkest days of life. Not only did he pick me up when I was down, but he also carried me through those dark lonely days. He never gave up on me, even though I lost my battle with grief so many times. Once again, my world has been torn apart. We came so far together, and through so much, side by side; from teenage love to 41 years of married life and a beautiful family, now here I stand alone again, where I started. The fear of being without my wonderful Alfie is almost unbearable.

One day, we came back from a weekend break with our family and my husband felt dizzy. It had been the anniversary of Naylor's death and we both thought it was a nervous feeling going through his body, but it went on too long. He had a blood test, and than a scan. This first scan showed shadows, and we both knew from then on it that it didn't look good and decided to tell our children. Our hearts were broken, but they had been through too much not to talk to them, so they were in from the start.

As we walked into the hospital doctor's room for the next meeting, an overwhelming feeling of fear overtook me, but the doctors were so kind and trying to be thoughtful, but when we were hit with the dreaded word 'cancer', our children ran out the room, leaving me and my husband looking at each other, asking questions and not remembering any of them. I felt devastated and my world dropped beneath me, and the look of disbelief on my husband's face sticks firmly in my mind. We were given the phone number of a Macmillan nurse and told that she could help us at any time, and then we walked to our car, my daughter, Phyllis, and our grandson, Naylor, crying because of what we had been told. I can remember thinking, 'why?' and feeling very weak.

A couple of weeks later we arrived back at the hospital to learn what type of cancer my husband had. We'd had time to try to get our heads around being told that Alfie had cancer and we were all trying to stay strong for him, just as he was so incredibly strong for us. We went in the consultant's room; Alfie, Naylor, Phyllis and her husband, Billy, for support, and as we walked in the door we could see chairs arranged in a horseshoe shape around the consultant's desk. My heart was pumping with fear for my husband and although I had lost my faith since the loss of my Naylor, how I prayed that there would be good news - but I knew in my heart that it wouldn't be good.

The consultant turned from his computer and greeted my husband. "Mr. Ball," he said. "You know you have cancer and I'm sorry to say, but it's terminal." I felt like saying, "Stop! No, this can't be! My poor Alfie has been the rock of our family. We love him so much - don't let him die. I need him - my children need him!" We all sat dumbstruck and then, my beautiful, brave husband struck up and said, "Well doctor, you need to tell me how long I have because I have a family and I need to put things in perspective and sort things out." "Three to four months, Alfie, and may be a year with trial drugs." We all sat, and I caught my husband's eye and fumbled for his hand. I will never forget the way he squeezed it tight to reassure me that it would be all right, like so many times before in our life. He was dying and still trying to comfort me. Just thinking of this makes me know how strong our love was, and I was thinking, "No! He's not old- he's only 58".

Our lives were in turmoil once again. My head was spinning and every time I looked at my husband I couldn't imagine how he was feeling. Our children were in disbelief and my husband knew it. He told me that once they got used to him being sick, then over time, the situation would help them to come to terms with him dying.

As the weeks passed, Alfie was getting weaker every day. He was given the trial drugs and I can remember the first time he took them. We got up really early, I gave him the tablets and sat with him, and as we were talking, I said, "You've got to stay strong, Alfie. We can do this together." He was holding my hand because I was crying, and I will never forget his words to me. "No. You've got to promise me that you are the one who is going to stay strong. I can't have you going back to the place where you were when we lost our Naylor." I could see the sadness in his eyes that had never left him since the loss of our beautiful son. "You've got to understand, my darling. There is going to be no silver lining to this," he said as he squeezed my hand. How true he was. Every time he got a week to ten days on the trial drug, he got knocked back down and had to stop it with stays in hospital. This was an ongoing thing throughout his illness, but although he was so ill, it didn't stop him from putting me and my children's lives on track. Throughout the following weeks, he planned most of his own funeral and by doing that he had made everything as easy as he could for me and the children. Coming from a Romany family, he knew how stressful things would get. When a member of our family dies, normally, as Romani, we start sitting up straight away when someone passes, but he changed that, to the amazement of me and our families.

He made it very clear that he didn't want any sitting up when he died. He told me that it would be too much for me and the children to deal with. It was hard for us to accept this and also that he didn't want to be brought home the night before his funeral. This upset my daughter, Phyllis, so much that she asked me to sit with her and try to talk to her dad.

We walked into the bedroom and Phyllis started the conversation by telling her dad that we were worried about the plans he had made. She was crying and told him how much we all loved and cared for him, and that it wasn't right for him not to be brought home to us the night before his funeral. "Whatever will the people think?" she said. This is an expression that Romanies have used for years when something goes wrong in their families, but who are these people? As my husband said, most of them are family and friends so they should understand. The conversation got very heated. Phyllis asked if it would be all right if we sat in the chapel of rest with him, but he was still adamant - "not all night."

I was sitting at the foot of the bed and he told me that on the night before his funeral he wanted his family at home, and his grandchildren all in their pyjamas and warm in bed. Phyllis kissed her dad and said, "Okay, we'll do it your way." She apologised and kept saying she was sorry for even questioning his wishes. He also told us that he wanted to be cremated, but he did compromise with me on one thing. I asked him if he could be brought home on the morning of the funeral and he agreed. It was so hard having this conversation and watching the man I loved so much dying and still trying to protect and care for his family.

Later, I learned that on that same day, when our friend, Terry Doe, had called round to visit my husband, Alfie had asked him, in confidence, to write the speech for his funeral. This must have been very hard for Terry because he was still in early days of recovery from cancer himself, but Alfie knew that Terry, his most trusted friend, would be the one to deliver his last important message to his family and friends at this unbearable time; my husband's own words about the morals he lived his life by, and for us to live the rest of ours.

154

On another day, whilst sitting with my husband I overheard a phone conversation to a close friend of his, Billy Redney. Billy was known as one of the best horsemen around and Alfie had the highest respect for Billy as a friend, and was arranging his last journey. It would be by a horse-drawn trolley, the same way that our son, Naylor, was carried to rest. It was heartbreaking to hear, but my husband was determined to sort things out himself. After the phone call, Alfie told me, "When I'm gone, just tell my Naylor to ring Billy, and he will sort it out." My husband sorted out every minor detail; he even had my door and gate keys colour-coded so I wouldn't get mixed up, and he bought me a smaller car and even a Tom-Tom, in case I needed to go on a journey. How strong and brave my husband was, thinking of his family right to the end.

The family was in turmoil, watching this strong man die, knowing that there was nothing we could do, and all our love couldn't save him. The next few weeks passed so quickly and our lives seem to spiral, not knowing which way to turn. The man we loved so much, the rock of our family was dying. How

Me, my Daughter and Alfie. The love he gave us was tremendous.

do you go on? I will tell you how you go on; you take strength from that person, whether it's my loved one or yours. In our case, my husband lay dying and was still trying to take care of and protect his family, so what right have we got to give up on each other? I found so much strength that I didn't know was there as I watched my husband die and the pain I suffered was unbearable. The love he gave and showed to his family was tremendous. He gave us hope, love, and the will to go on. He was our angel, our everything. Sadly, my beautiful Alfie had no choice but to let go. With his close family around him, holding his hand and telling him how much we loved him, he left this world and I believe my son, Naylor, came and took his hand and showed him the way to a better place than where we are..

My husband achieved so many goals in his life, but the one dearest to his heart was taking on our grandson, Naylor, so young and lost, and so full of grief, and watching him grow into a remarkably strong young man. They started a journey together through blood, sweat and tears in Naylor's boxing career, which they both enjoyed so much, and since losing his grandad, my grandson has been given a three-

Life was hard without his grandad by his side.

year contract, and turned pro with one of the world's topmost boxing promoters. This was so very hard for Naylor not having his granddad by his side at this important time of his life, but Alfie taught him that through life you take the pain and turn it into strength. His granddad would be so proud of him.

Naylor living his Dad's and Grandad's dreams.

These are the words that Alfie asked Terry to say at the funeral:

"Of course I'd love to be with you, but that can't be, so we've got to get on with it, like we've always done. I know you can do it.

Please love one another, look after one another and forgive one another, because when it comes down to it, we're all we've got and this time is such a precious thing, so please don't waste a minute of it and never forget how proud I am of all of you.

Above all, please take care of each other like you took care of me, and you'll all be OK I promise."

The last farewell.

This is the legacy that my Alfie left us; being part of his life and loving him has made us strong and able to go on.

Printed in the United States
By Bookmasters